DEVELOPING
VIDEO GAME
USING PYGAME, ARCADE
AND PANDA 3D

Mastering Python Game
Development from 2D to
3D Game Design

RICHARD D. CROWLEY

Table of Contents

Part I: **14**

Foundations of Python Game Development   **14**

CHAPTER 1   **15**

Introduction to Python Game Development and Framework Selection 15

1.1 The Landscape of Python Game Development   16

1.2 Understanding Game Development Concepts   20

1.3 Introduction to Pygame, Arcade, and Panda3D   23

1.4 Choosing the Right Framework for Your Project   27

1.5 Setting Up Your Development Environment (Python, IDE, Libraries) 31

1.6 Best Practices for Python Game Development   34

CHAPTER 2   **39**

Python Fundamentals for Game Development   39

2.1 Review of Essential Python Concepts (Variables, Data Types, Loops, Functions)   40

Before we embark on the journey of building games, it's essential to solidify our understanding of Python's core elements. These are the building blocks upon which all game logic and mechanics will be constructed.   40

2.2 Object-Oriented Programming (OOP) in Python for Games   44

2.3 Working with Modules and Libraries 49

2.4 Error Handling and Debugging Techniques   53

2.5 Introduction to Game-Specific Data Structures (Vectors, Matrices)   58

Part II: **62**

2D Game Development with Pygame 62

CHAPTER 3   **63**

Building Basic 2D Games with Pygame 63

3.1 Pygame Initialization and Game Loop Structure   64

3.2 Drawing and Displaying Graphics   71

3.3 Handling User Input (Keyboard, Mouse) 75

3.4 Working with Sprites and Images 80

3.5 Basic Game Logic and Event Handling 84

3.6 Creating a Simple Game Example (e.g., a simple pong game) 87

CHAPTER 4 **89**

Advanced 2D Game Mechanics and Features in Pygame 89

4.1 Implementing Collision Detection 89

4.2 Adding Sound and Music 95

4.3 Animation Techniques and Sprite Sheets 101

4.4 Implementing Game States and Menus 104

4.5 Working with Text and Fonts 109

4.6 Optimization and Performance Considerations 112

CHAPTER 5 **116**

Building a Complete 2D Game Project with Pygame 116

5.1 Project Planning and Design 117

5.2 Developing Core Game Mechanics 120

5.3 Creating Levels and Game Assets 123

5.4 Implementing User Interface (UI) Elements 127

5.5 Testing, Debugging, and Polishing Your Game 132

5.6 Distributing Your Pygame Application 136

Part III: **140**

Streamlining 2D Development with Arcade **140**

CHAPTER 6 **141**

Introduction to Arcade: Modern 2D Game Development 141

6.1 Arcade Framework Overview and Advantages 142

6.2 Setting Up and Using Arcade 146

6.3 Arcade's Structure and Game Window Management 150

6.4 Simplified Sprite Management and Collision Handling 154

6.5 Introduction to Arcade's Built-in Physics Engine 157

CHAPTER 7 **161**

Advanced Arcade Features and Game DesignArcade provides powerful features for creating sophisticated 2D games, including: 161

7.1 Leveraging Arcade's Scene Management 162

7.2 Advanced Sprite Animation and Effects 166

7.3 Creating Complex Game Mechanics with Arcade's Physics 172

7.4 Using Arcade's Tiled Map Support 174

7.5 Implementing Advanced UI and GUI Elements: Enhancing User Interaction 179

7.6 Building a Platformer Game Example using Arcade: Putting it All Together 183

Part IV: 187

Transitioning to 3D with Panda3D 187

CHAPTER 8 188

Introduction to 3D Game Development and Panda3D 188

8.1 Understanding 3D Game Development Concepts (Vertices, Polygons, Textures) 188

8.2 Panda3D Framework Overview and Architecture 192

8.3 Setting Up Panda3D and Understanding its Scene Graph 195

8.4 Loading and Manipulating 3D Models 198

8.5 Basic 3D Rendering and Camera Control 204

8.6 Essential 3D Math for Game Development 209

CHAPTER 9 **211**

Advanced 3D Game Mechanics in Panda3D 211

9.1 Implementing 3D Collision Detection and Physics 211

9.2 Working with Lighting and Shaders 217

9.3 Creating and Applying Textures and Materials 220

9.4 Animating 3D Models and Characters 223

9.5 Implementing 3D Audio and Sound Effects 228

9.6 Creating a 3D Scene Example 229

CHAPTER 10 **236**

User Interaction and Game Logic in 3D Environments 236

10.1 Handling 3D User Input (Mouse, Keyboard, Gamepad): The Player's Voice

236

10.2 Implementing Game Logic and State Management in 3D: The Game's Brain 245

10.3 Creating Interactive 3D Environments 252

Interactive 3D environments are the soul of engaging games. They allow players to feel immersed and connected to the game world, fostering a sense of presence and agency. 252

10.4 Building 3D User Interfaces (UI): Bridging the Gap 258

10.5 Implementing AI and Pathfinding in 3D Games: Smart Enemies and Dynamic Worlds 262

Part V: **267**

Comprehensive 3D Game Project and Deployment **267**

CHAPTER 11 **268**

Designing and Developing a Complete 3D Game Project with Panda3D 268

11.1 Project Planning and 3D Game Design: Laying the Groundwork 268

11.2 Creating 3D Game Assets and Environments: Building the World 272

11.3 Implementing Core 3D Game Mechanics 278

11.4 Optimizing Performance for 3D Games: Smooth and Responsive Gameplay 285

11.5 Testing, Debugging, and Polishing Your 3D Game: Ensuring Quality and Polish 289

CHAPTER 12 **293**

Advanced Panda3D Techniques and Optimization Advanced Panda3D techniques and optimization are crucial for creating visually stunning and performant 3D games. These techniques allow developers to push the boundaries of visual fidelity and create immersive experiences that captivate players. 293

12.1 Using Panda3D's Particle Systems: Adding Dynamic Visuals 293

12.2 Implementing Advanced Shaders and Visual Effects: Enhancing Visual Realism 299

12.3 Profiling and Optimizing Panda3D Applications 304

12.4 Integrating External Libraries and Plugins: Extending Functionality 310

12.5 Creating Networked 3D Games (Basic Concepts): Connecting Players 314

CHAPTER 13   **318**

Cross-Platform   Deployment   and
Distribution   318

13.1 Packaging Pygame, Arcade, and
Panda3D   Games: Preparing   for
Distribution   328

13.2 Creating Executable Files for
Windows,   macOS,   and   Linux:
Platform-Specific Distributions   324

13.3 Distributing Games on Game
Platforms (Steam, Itch.io)   329

13.4   Mobile   Game   Development
Considerations   (If   Applicable):
Expanding to Mobile   334

CHAPTER 14   **340**

Game   Design   Principles   and   Best
Practices   340

14.1 Understanding Core Game Design
Principles: Foundations of Engagement
340

14.2 Level Design and Player Experience:
Crafting Engaging Worlds   347

14.3 Storytelling and Narrative in Games
352

14.4   Monetization   Strategies   (If
Applicable): Generating Revenue   358

14.5 Building a Game Development
Portfolio: Showcasing Your Skills   362

CHAPTER 15   **366**

Future   Trends   in   Python   Game
Development   366

15.1 Emerging Technologies (VR/AR,
Cloud   Gaming):   Expanding   the
Boundaries of Immersion   366

15.2 Advances in Game Engines and
Libraries: Empowering Python Game
Development   371

15.3 The Role of Python in Future Game
Development   376

15.4 Community and Resources for
Continued Learning: Fostering Growth
and Collaboration   384

Conclusion   **390**

Recap of Key Concepts and Skills
Learned: A Foundation for Future
Innovation   390

The   Future   of   Python   Game
Development: A Promising Horizon 395

Appendix   **398**

A.1: Python Quick Reference: A Concise Guide to Core Concepts   398

A.2: Pygame, Arcade, and Panda3D API Summaries: Essential Functionality   401

A.3: Game Asset Resources and Tools: Enhancing Your Creations   404

A.4: Troubleshooting Common Issues 408

A.5: Glossary of Game Development Terms: Deciphering the Developer's Lexicon   419

Part I:

Foundations of Python Game Development

CHAPTER 1

Introduction to Python Game Development and Framework Selection

Python, with its readability and versatility, offers a compelling avenue for game development.[1] While not a powerhouse for AAA titles, its strength lies in rapid prototyping, indie development, and educational use.[2] The landscape encompasses libraries like Pygame (for foundational 2D), Arcade (for streamlined, modern 2D), and Panda3D (for robust 3D).

Choosing the right framework hinges on project scope, complexity, and desired features. Pygame is beginner-friendly and great for simple 2D, Arcade excels in more complex 2D projects, and Panda3D is essential for 3D games.[3] Setting up a proper development environment (Python, IDE, virtual environments, libraries) is crucial.[4] Best practices include organized code, optimized game loops, efficient asset management, robust error handling, and version control. Ultimately, understanding the core concepts and carefully selecting a framework are the first steps towards successful Python game development.

1.1 The Landscape of Python Game Development

Python, often hailed for its readability and versatility, has carved a niche in the realm of game development.[1] While it might not be the powerhouse behind AAA titles, its simplicity and robust libraries make it an excellent choice for indie developers, educational purposes, and rapid prototyping.[2]

- **A Historical Perspective:**

- Python's adoption in game development has evolved.[3] Initially, it was often used for scripting and tool development within larger game engines. However, the emergence of libraries like Pygame democratized game creation, allowing individuals to build complete games from scratch.
- The rise of indie game development has further fueled Python's popularity. Its ease of use lowers the barrier to entry, enabling creators to focus on game design and mechanics rather than intricate coding.[4]
- **Python's Strengths in Game Development:**
  - **Readability and Ease of Learning:** Python's syntax is beginner-friendly, making it ideal for those new to

programming or game development.[5]

- **Rapid Prototyping:** Python's dynamic nature allows for quick iterations and experimentation, crucial for game development's iterative process.[6]

- **Cross-Platform Compatibility:** Python runs on various operating systems, simplifying game deployment.[7]

- **Extensive Libraries:** A wealth of libraries, including those we'll discuss, provides pre-built functionalities, saving development time.

- **Community Support:** A vibrant community offers ample resources, tutorials, and support for Python game developers.[8]

- **Python's Limitations in Game Development:**
  - **Performance:** Python's interpreted nature can lead to

performance bottlenecks, especially in graphically intensive 3D games.[9]

- Garbage Collection: Python's automatic memory management might introduce occasional pauses, affecting real-time performance.
- Limited AAA Industry Adoption: While Python is used in some aspects of larger game studios, it's not a primary language for AAA game engines.

- **The Role of Python in Different Game Genres:**
  - Python excels in 2D games, puzzle games, strategy games, and visual novels.
  - It's also suitable for educational games, simulations, and experimental projects.
  - While 3D games are possible, careful optimization and

framework selection are
essential.

1.2 Understanding Game Development Concepts

Before diving into specific frameworks, it's
crucial to grasp fundamental game
development concepts.

- **The Game Loop:**
  - The heart of every game, the
    game loop continuously updates
    and renders the game state.[10]
  - It typically consists of:
    - **Input Handling:**
      Processing user input
      (keyboard, mouse, etc.).
    - **Game Logic:** Updating
      game variables,
      implementing game rules,
      and handling collisions.

- **Rendering:** Drawing the game state to the screen.
- **Sprites:**
  - 2D images or animations used to represent game objects.[11]
  - They are fundamental building blocks for 2D games.
- **Collision Detection:**
  - Detecting when two game objects intersect.
  - Essential for implementing interactions, combat, and physics.
- **Game States:**
  - Different modes of the game (e.g., menu, gameplay, pause).
  - Managing game states ensures a structured and organized game flow.
- **Event Handling:**
  - Responding to user actions and system events.
  - Essential for creating interactive and responsive games.

- **Rendering Techniques:**
  - **2D Rendering:** Drawing 2D images and shapes to the screen.
  - **3D Rendering:** Projecting 3D models onto a 2D screen.[12]
  - **Vertexes, Polygons, Textures:** The basic building blocks of 3D rendering.
- **Physics Engines:**
  - Simulating realistic physical interactions.
  - Essential for creating believable game worlds.
- **Audio and Sound Effects:**
  - Adding sound to enhance immersion and provide feedback.
- **User Interface (UI):**
  - Creating interactive elements for menus, settings, and in-game displays.
- **Game Design Principles:**
  - Understanding core design principles like player experience,

level design, and game mechanics.

1.3 Introduction to Pygame, Arcade, and Panda3D

These three libraries offer distinct approaches to Python game development, catering to different needs and skill levels.[13]

- **Pygame:**
    - A cross-platform set of Python modules designed for writing video games.[14]
    - Known for its simplicity and ease of use, making it ideal for beginners.[15]
    - Provides functionalities for graphics, sound, input, and basic game logic.[16]
    - Offers a low-level approach, giving developers greater control over game mechanics.

- Excellent for 2D games, especially those with retro or pixel art styles.
- **Arcade:**
  - A modern 2D game framework built on top of Pygame.
  - Designed to simplify 2D game development with a more structured and intuitive API.[17]
  - Offers features like sprite batching, built-in physics, and Tiled map support.[18]
  - Provides a more streamlined workflow, reducing boilerplate code.[19]
  - Great for platformers, and other 2D games that would benefit from better organisation.
- **Panda3D:**
  - A 3D game engine developed by Disney Interactive.
  - Provides a comprehensive set of tools for creating 3D games and simulations.

- Offers advanced features like scene graph management, lighting, shaders, and physics.
- Suitable for creating complex 3D environments and games.
- Has a steeper learning curve than Pygame or Arcade.
- Powerful for those who wish to create 3D games with python.

Key Considerations When Choosing a Framework:

- **Project Scope:**
  - For simple 2D games, Pygame or Arcade might suffice.
  - For complex 3D games, Panda3D is a better choice.
- **Skill Level:**
  - Pygame is excellent for beginners.[20]
  - Arcade is good for those that have some experience, and want

a more modern approach to 2D games.

- ○ Panda3D requires a deeper understanding of 3D concepts.
- **Performance Requirements:**
  - ○ Panda3D offers better performance for 3D games.
- **Features and Functionality:**
  - ○ Consider the specific features needed for your game.
  - ○ Arcade offers better physics and tilemap support than pygame.
  - ○ Panda3D offers far greater 3D functionality than the other two.
- **Community and Support:**
  - ○ A strong community provides valuable resources and assistance.[21]

By understanding these core concepts and carefully evaluating your project requirements, you can make an informed decision when selecting a Python game development framework.

1.4 Choosing the Right Framework for Your Project

Selecting the appropriate framework is paramount to a successful game development journey. It's not merely a matter of technical preference; it's about aligning the tool with the project's vision and constraints.

- **Project Scope and Complexity:**
  - **Simple 2D Games:** If you're creating a simple 2D game like a platformer, a puzzle game, or a retro-style arcade game, Pygame or Arcade are excellent choices.[1] Pygame offers a foundational approach, while Arcade provides a more structured and modern workflow.

- **Complex 2D Games:** If you need advanced physics, tile-based maps, or sophisticated animation, Arcade's features become highly advantageous.
- **3D Games:** For 3D games, Panda3D is the clear frontrunner. Its robust 3D rendering capabilities, scene graph management, and physics engine make it suitable for creating immersive 3D environments.
- **Target Platform:**
  - Consider where you intend to deploy your game. Pygame, Arcade, and Panda3D are cross-platform, but specific features or performance considerations might vary across operating systems.
  - If mobile deployment is a goal, research specific mobile support within the chosen framework.

- **Performance Requirements:**
  - Python's inherent performance limitations should be considered.
  - For graphically intensive 3D games, Panda3D's C++ core provides a performance boost compared to pure Python libraries.[2]
  - Arcade has performance enhancements over Pygame. If your 2D game needs high performance, Arcade is a good choice.
- **Learning Curve:**
  - Pygame has a relatively shallow learning curve, making it accessible to beginners.[3]
  - Arcade builds upon Pygame, offering a more streamlined API, but requires some familiarity with game development concepts.

- Panda3D has a steeper learning curve, especially for those new to 3D graphics and game development.
- **Community and Support:**
  - A strong community provides invaluable resources, tutorials, and support.[4]
  - Pygame has a large and established community, while Arcade and Panda3D have growing communities.
  - Consider the availability of documentation and online forums.
- **Development Speed:**
  - Arcade's streamlined API and built-in features can accelerate development time compared to Pygame.
  - Pygame gives the developer much more control, but that control comes at the cost of development time.

- **Personal Preferences and Experience:**
  - Ultimately, the choice of framework depends on your personal preferences and experience.
  - Experiment with different frameworks to find the one that best suits your coding style and workflow.

1.5 Setting Up Your Development Environment (Python, IDE, Libraries)

A well-configured development environment is essential for a smooth and productive game development experience.

- **Python Installation:**
  - Download and install the latest stable version of Python from

the official Python website (python.org).[5]

- Ensure that you add Python to your system's PATH environment variable.

- **Integrated Development Environment (IDE):**
  - An IDE provides a comprehensive set of tools for coding, debugging, and testing.[6]
  - Popular IDEs for Python game development include:
    - **Visual Studio Code (VS Code):** A lightweight and highly customizable IDE with excellent Python support.
    - **PyCharm:** A dedicated Python IDE with advanced features for code completion, debugging, and project management.[7]

- **IDLE:** The default python IDE, and a great place to start.
  - Choose an IDE that aligns with your preferences and workflow.
- **Virtual Environments:**
  - Create a virtual environment to isolate your project's dependencies.
  - This prevents conflicts between different projects and ensures that your game runs consistently.
  - Use venv or conda to create and manage virtual environments.
- **Library Installation:**
  - Use pip (Python's package installer) to install the necessary libraries:
    - pip install pygame
    - pip install arcade
    - pip install panda3d

- Install any other required libraries, such as NumPy, Pillow, or PyOpenGL.
- **Asset Management:**
  - Organize your game assets (images, sounds, models) in a structured manner.
  - Use version control (e.g., Git) to track changes to your assets and code.
- **Graphics Drivers:**
  - Ensure that your graphics drivers are up to date, especially for 3D game development with Panda3D.

1.6 Best Practices for Python Game Development

Adhering to best practices enhances code quality, maintainability, and performance.

- **Code Organization:**

- Structure your code into logical modules and classes.
- Follow the principles of object-oriented programming (OOP) to create reusable and maintainable code.
- Use clear and descriptive variable and function names.

- **Game Loop Optimization:**
  - Optimize your game loop to minimize processing overhead.
  - Use profiling tools to identify performance bottlenecks.
  - Implement techniques like sprite batching and culling to improve rendering performance.

- **Collision Detection Optimization:**
  - Use efficient collision detection algorithms, such as bounding boxes or circle collisions.
  - Minimize the number of collision checks performed per frame.

- **Asset Optimization:**
  - Optimize your game assets to reduce file size and loading times.
  - Use appropriate image and audio formats.
  - Use sprite sheets to minimize draw calls.
- **Error Handling:**
  - Implement robust error handling to prevent crashes.
  - Use try-except blocks to catch and handle exceptions.
  - Log errors for debugging purposes.
- **Code Documentation:**
  - Document your code with clear and concise comments.
  - Use docstrings to describe the purpose and usage of functions and classes.
- **Version Control:**
  - Use version control (e.g., Git) to track changes to your code.

- ○ Commit your code regularly and use descriptive commit messages.
- **Testing and Debugging:**
  - ○ Test your game thoroughly to identify and fix bugs.
  - ○ Use debugging tools to step through your code and inspect variables.
  - ○ Write unit tests to verify the correctness of your code.
- **Performance Profiling:**
  - ○ Use profiling tools to identify areas of your game that are slow.
  - ○ Optimize those areas to improve performance.
- **Community Engagement:**
  - ○ Engage with the Python game development community.
  - ○ Share your knowledge and learn from others.
  - ○ Contribute to open-source projects.

By following these best practices, you can create high-quality Python games that are both enjoyable to play and maintainable over time.

CHAPTER 2

Python Fundamentals for Game Development

A strong foundation in core Python concepts is vital for effective game development. This includes a thorough understanding of:

- **Variables and Data Types:** To represent and manipulate game state (player health, positions, etc.).
- **Control Flow (if/else, loops):** To implement game logic and manage game loops.
- **Functions:** For code organization, reusability, and modular design.
- **Object-Oriented Programming (OOP):** To structure game entities and their interactions through classes, objects, inheritance, and polymorphism.

Mastery of these elements enables developers to create structured, maintainable, and engaging game experiences. OOP, in particular, facilitates the creation of complex, interactive game worlds by modeling game elements as distinct objects with defined behaviors.

2.1 Review of Essential Python Concepts (Variables, Data Types, Loops, Functions)

Before we embark on the journey of building games, it's essential to solidify our understanding of Python's core elements. These are the building blocks upon which all game logic and mechanics will be constructed.

- **Variables and Data Types:**
    - Variables are containers for storing data.[1] In game development, they represent

everything from player positions to game scores.

- Understanding data types is crucial:
  - **Integers (int):** Whole numbers (e.g., player health, score).
  - **Floats (float):** Decimal numbers (e.g., player speed, coordinates).[2]
  - **Strings (str):** Textual data (e.g., player names, game messages).[3]
  - **Booleans (bool):** True or False values (e.g., is_player_alive, is_game_over).[4]
  - **Lists (list):** Ordered collections of items (e.g., enemy positions, inventory).[5]
  - **Tuples (tuple):** Immutable ordered collections (e.g.,

coordinates, fixed game settings).[6]

- **Dictionaries (dict):** Key-value pairs (e.g., player stats, game settings).[7]

o In game development, lists and dictionaries are extremely useful for storing and manipulating game data.

- **Loops:**
    o Loops allow us to repeat blocks of code, essential for game loops, animation, and repetitive tasks.[8]
    o **For Loops:** Iterate over a sequence (e.g., a list of enemies, a range of numbers).[9]
        - Used to process each sprite in a list, or to cycle through a sequence of animations.
    o

- While Loops: Repeat a block of code as long as a condition is true.[10]
  - The core of the game loop itself, and useful for repeating actions until a specific condition is met.
  -

- **Functions:**
  - Functions are reusable blocks of code that perform specific tasks.[11]
  - They promote code organization, modularity, and reusability.
  - In game development, functions are used for:
    - Handling player input.
    - Updating game logic.
    - Drawing game elements.
    - Managing game states.
  - Functions help to break down large and complex game logic

into smaller, more manageable pieces.

- ○ Functions can return values, which is extremely important for data manipulation.[12]

2.2 Object-Oriented Programming (OOP) in Python for Games

OOP is a paradigm that structures code around objects, which encapsulate data and behavior.[13] It's particularly well-suited for game development, where entities and interactions are naturally modeled as objects.

- **Classes and Objects:**
  - ○ A class is a blueprint for creating objects.
  - ○ An object is an instance of a class.[14]
  - ○ In games, classes can represent:

- Players.
- Enemies.
- Projectiles.
- Game levels.
- UI elements.
  - By using classes, we can create many instances of similar game entities, each with their own unique properties and behaviors.
- **Encapsulation:**
  - Bundling data and methods within a class, hiding internal implementation details.
  - This promotes data integrity and reduces the risk of unintended modifications.
  - For example, a player class might encapsulate its health, position, and movement logic, preventing other parts of the code from directly manipulating these attributes.
- **Inheritance:**

- Creating new classes (derived classes) that inherit properties and methods from existing classes (base classes).
- This promotes code reuse[15] and allows for creating specialized objects.
- For example, we might have a base Enemy class and derived classes like Goblin and Dragon, each with specific attributes and behaviors.

- **Polymorphism:**
  - The ability of objects to take on multiple forms.
  - This allows for writing generic code that can work with different types of objects.
  - For example, a draw() method might be implemented differently for different game objects, allowing them to be rendered appropriately.

- **Benefits of OOP in Game Development:**
  - **Modularity:** Breaking down complex game logic into smaller, manageable objects.
  - **Reusability:** Creating reusable classes and objects.
  - **Maintainability:** Easier to modify and extend game code.
  - **Organization:** Structuring game code in a logical and intuitive way.
  - **Scalability:** Handling large and complex game projects.
- **Example of OOP in a Game:**
  - Imagine a game with a Player class:
    - Attributes: health, position, speed.
    - Methods: move(), attack(), take_damage().
  - Then, an Enemy class:
    - Attributes: health, position, attack_power.

- Methods: move(), attack(), take_damage().
  - And a Projectile class:
    - Attributes: position, speed, damage.
    - Methods: move(), check_collision().
  - These classes can interact with each other, creating a dynamic and engaging game world.

By mastering these fundamental Python concepts and embracing the power of OOP, you'll be well-equipped to create robust, well-structured, and engaging games.

2.3 Working with Modules and Libraries

Python's strength lies in its extensive standard library and vast ecosystem of third-party modules.[1] Mastering how to work with them is essential for efficient game development.

- **Modules: Organizing and Reusing Code**
  - Modules are Python files containing functions, classes, and variables.[2] They allow you to organize your code into logical units and reuse it across multiple projects.[3]
  - **Importing Modules:**
    - import module_name: Imports the entire module.
    - from module_name import function_name:

Imports specific functions or classes.

- `import module_name as alias`: Imports a module with a shorter alias.

- **Standard Library Modules:**
    - Python's standard library provides a wealth of modules for various tasks, including:
        - `math`: Mathematical functions (e.g., trigonometric functions, logarithms).
        - `random`: Generating random numbers (e.g., for enemy behavior, item drops).
        - `time`: Working with time (e.g., for game timers, animations).

- **os**: Interacting with the operating system (e.g., file management).
- Understanding these modules can significantly reduce development time.
- **Third-Party Libraries:**
  - Libraries like Pygame, Arcade, and Panda3D are essential for game development.[4]
  - Other useful libraries include:
    - NumPy: For numerical computations and array manipulation (essential for game-specific data structures).
    - Pillow (PIL): For image processing.

- **PyOpenGL:** For low-level OpenGL graphics programming.
- **Sounddevice:** For advanced audio manipulation.
- Using these libraries allows you to leverage existing functionality and avoid reinventing the wheel.
  - **Creating Your Own Modules:**
    - Organizing your game code into modules promotes modularity and reusability.[5]
    - Create modules for specific game components, such as:
      - player.py: Player-related

functions and classes.

- enemy.py: Enemy-related functions and classes.
- level.py: Level loading and management.
- This helps keep your main game file clean and organized.

2.4 Error Handling and Debugging Techniques

Errors are inevitable in game development. Mastering error handling and debugging is crucial for creating robust and stable games.

- **Error Handling (try-except Blocks):**

- ○ try-except blocks allow you to catch and handle exceptions (errors) that occur during runtime.
- ○ This prevents your game from crashing and allows you to provide informative error messages.
- ○ Example:
- ○ Python

```
try:
    # Code that might raise an exception
    result = 10 / 0
except ZeroDivisionError:
    print("Error: Division by zero")
```

- ○
- ○

- Specific   Exception **Handling:**
  - Catch specific exceptions to handle different error types appropriately.
  - Common exceptions in game development include:
    - FileNotFoundError: When a game asset cannot be loaded.
    - TypeError: When an operation is performed on an incompatible data type.
    - IndexError: When accessing an invalid index in a list.
- **Logging:**
  - Use the logging module to record errors and other important events.

- Logging provides a history of your game's execution, which can be invaluable for debugging.
- By logging information to a file, you can track down bugs that only occur during long play sessions.
- **Debugging Techniques:**
  - **Print Statements:**
    - Use print() statements to inspect variable values and trace the flow of execution.
    - While simple, this technique can be effective for identifying basic errors.
  - **Debugging Tools (IDEs):**
    - IDEs like VS Code and PyCharm provide powerful debugging tools, including:[6]

- Breakpoints: Pause execution at specific lines of code.[7]
- Step-through debugging: Execute code line by line.[8]
- Variable inspection: Examine the values of variables during runtime.
- ■
- Learning to use these tools can significantly speed up the debugging process.
- **Assertions:**
  - The assert statement tests if a condition is true. If it is false, the program stops.
  - Useful for checking that game variables are within expected ranges.
- **Rubber Duck Debugging:**
  - Explaining your code to someone (or something,

like a rubber duck) can
help you identify errors
that you might have
overlooked.
- ■ The act of articulating your
  code's logic can often
  reveal flaws in your
  thinking.

2.5   Introduction   to Game-Specific Data Structures (Vectors, Matrices)

Game development often involves working with spatial data and transformations.[9] Understanding game-specific data structures is essential.

- • **Vectors:**
  - ○ Vectors represent direction and magnitude.[10]

- In 2D games, vectors are used to represent:
    - Player position.
    - Object velocity.
    - Direction of movement.
- In 3D games, vectors are used to represent:
    - 3D coordinates.
    - Normals (surface directions).
    - Camera directions.
- **Vector Operations:**
    - Addition, subtraction, dot product, cross product, normalization.
    - These operations are fundamental for game physics, collision detection, and transformations.
- **NumPy Arrays:**
    - NumPy arrays are ideal for representing vectors and matrices.[11]

- They provide efficient array operations and mathematical functions.
- **Matrices:**
  - Matrices are used to represent linear transformations, such as:
    - Rotation.
    - Scaling.
    - Translation.
  - In 3D games, matrices are used to transform 3D models and camera views.[12]
  - **Matrix Operations:**
    - Matrix multiplication, inversion, transposition.
  - **Transformations:**
    - Understanding how to use matrices to transform game objects is essential for 3D game development.
- **Game-Specific Data Structures:**
  - **Bounding Boxes:**
    - Rectangular regions used for collision detection.

- **Collision Masks:**
  - Pixel-perfect collision detection.
- **Quadtrees/Octrees:**
  - Data structures for efficient spatial partitioning.
- **Graphs:**
  - Used for pathfinding and AI.

By mastering these concepts, you'll be well-prepared to tackle the challenges of game development and create engaging and robust games.

Part II:

2D Game Development with Pygame

CHAPTER 3

Building Basic 2D Games with Pygame

Pygame provides the tools to create 2D games by focusing on core elements:

- **Initialization and Game Loop:** Setting up the game environment and managing the flow of the game through event handling, logic updates, and rendering.
- **Graphics and Sprites:** Drawing shapes, loading images, and utilizing sprites for game objects and animations.
- **User Input:** Handling keyboard and mouse input to create interactive gameplay.
- **Game Logic and Event Handling:** Implementing rules and responding to player actions and game events.

- **Simple Game Examples:** Practical application of concepts through basic games like Pong, reinforcing fundamental skills.

By mastering these areas, developers can create functional and engaging 2D games using Pygame.

3.1 Pygame Initialization and Game Loop Structure

The foundation of any Pygame game lies in its initialization and the game loop. These elements establish the environment and control the flow of your game.

- **Pygame Initialization (pygame.init()):**
  - Before using any Pygame functions, you must initialize the library.[1]

- pygame.init() initializes all imported Pygame modules. It's crucial to call this at the beginning of your game.
- It sets up the necessary resources for graphics, sound, and input handling.[2]
- It is good practice to check if the initialization was successful.
- **Creating the Game Window (pygame.display.set_mode()):**
  - This function creates the game window where your graphics will be displayed.[3]
  - You specify the window's dimensions (width and height) as a tuple.[4]
  - Example: screen = pygame.display.set_mode((800, 600)) creates an 800x600 pixel window.
  - You can also specify display flags, such as

pygame.FULLSCREEN or pygame.RESIZABLE.

- pygame.display.set_caption() sets the window title.

- **The Game Loop (The Heart of the Game):**
  - The game loop is a continuous cycle that processes input, updates game logic, and renders graphics.[5]
  - It's typically implemented using a while loop that runs as long as the game is running.
  - **Structure of a Basic Game Loop:**
    1. **Event Handling:**
       - Process user input (keyboard, mouse, etc.) and system events (window close).[6]
       - pygame.event.get() retrieves a list of

events that have occurred.

- Handle events like pygame.QUIT (window close), pygame.KEYDOWN (key press), and pygame.MOUSEBUTTONDOWN (mouse click).

2. **Game Logic Updates:**

- Update game variables, move objects, check for collisions, and implement game rules.
- This is where you implement the core mechanics of your game.

3. **Rendering:**

- Draw graphics to the screen.

- Use Pygame's drawing functions to draw shapes, images, and text.[7]
- screen.fill() clears the screen with a background color.
- screen.blit() draws images onto the screen.
- pygame.display.flip() or pygame.display.update() updates the display to show the rendered graphics.

4. **Frame Rate Control:**
   - Control the speed of the game loop to ensure consistent gameplay.
   - pygame.time.Clock() creates a clock object.

- clock.tick(fps) limits the frame rate to the specified frames per second (fps).
- This prevents the game from running too fast or too slow on different computers.
  - **Example Game Loop Snippet:**
  - Python

```python
import pygame

pygame.init()
screen = pygame.display.set_mode((800, 600))
pygame.display.set_caption("My Pygame Window")
clock = pygame.time.Clock()
running = True
```

```
while running:
    for event in pygame.event.get():
        if event.type == pygame.QUIT:
            running = False

    # Game logic updates here

        screen.fill((0, 0, 0)) #fill screen with
black.

    # Rendering here

    pygame.display.flip()
    clock.tick(60)

pygame.quit()
```

○

○

3.2 Drawing and Displaying Graphics

Pygame provides a set of powerful functions for drawing and displaying graphics, allowing you to create visually appealing games.[8]

- **Drawing Shapes:**
    - pygame.draw.rect(): Draws rectangles.
    - pygame.draw.circle(): Draws circles.
    - pygame.draw.polygon(): Draws polygons.
    - pygame.draw.line(): Draws lines.
    - pygame.draw.ellipse(): Draws ellipses.
    - These functions take arguments for the surface to draw on, color, position, and size.[9]
    - You can specify the fill color and line thickness.

- **Working with Images (Sprites):**
  - Images are essential for representing game objects.
  - pygame.image.load() loads an image from a file.
  - screen.blit() draws an image onto the screen.
  - **Sprites:**
    - Sprites are 2D images used to represent game objects.[10]
    - Pygame's pygame.sprite.Sprite class provides a base class for creating sprites.
    - You can create sprite groups to manage multiple sprites efficiently.
    - **Sprite Sheets:**
      - Sprite sheets contain multiple images arranged in a grid.[11]
      - They are used to optimize animation

and reduce file loading.
- You can extract individual images from a sprite sheet using slicing techniques.

- **Colors:**
  - Colors are represented as RGB tuples (red, green, blue).[12]
  - Example: (255, 0, 0) is red, (0, 255, 0) is green, (0, 0, 255) is blue, and (255,255,255) is white.
  - You can also use predefined colors from pygame.Color.

- **Text Rendering:**
  - pygame.font.Font() loads a font from a file or system font.
  - font.render() renders text onto a surface.
  - screen.blit() draws the rendered text onto the screen.
  - You can specify the font size, color, and style.

- **Surface Operations:**
  - screen.fill(): Fills the surface with a color.
  - screen.blit(): Draws one surface onto another.
  - pygame.transform.scale(): Resizes a surface.
  - pygame.transform.rotate(): Rotates a surface.
  - pygame.transform.flip(): Flips a surface horizontally or vertically.
- **Drawing Order:**
  - The order in which you draw graphics matters.
  - Graphics drawn later will appear on top of graphics drawn earlier.
  - Use layers or sprite groups to control the drawing order.

By mastering these fundamental concepts of Pygame initialization, game loops, and graphics rendering, you'll be well on your way to creating your own 2D games.

3.3 Handling User Input (Keyboard, Mouse)

Interactivity is at the heart of any engaging game. Pygame provides robust mechanisms for capturing and responding to user input from the keyboard and mouse.

- **Keyboard Input:**
  - pygame.key.get_pressed(): This function returns a sequence of boolean values representing the state of each key on the keyboard.
  - If a key is pressed, its corresponding value in the sequence is True; otherwise, it's False.
  - You can use pygame.K_ constants (e.g.,

pygame.K_LEFT,
pygame.K_SPACE,
pygame.K_a) to identify specific
keys.
- Example:
- Python

```
keys = pygame.key.get_pressed()
if keys[pygame.K_LEFT]:
    # Move player left
    player_x -= player_speed
if keys[pygame.K_SPACE]:
    # Player jumps
    # ...
```

-
-
- **Event-Based   Keyboard
  Handling:**

- Alternatively, you can handle keyboard input using events:
  - pygame.KEYDOWN: Triggered when a key is pressed.
  - pygame.KEYUP: Triggered when a key is released.
- This approach is more precise and allows you to capture key presses and releases individually.
- Example:
- Python

```
for event in pygame.event.get():
    if event.type == pygame.KEYDOWN:
        if event.key == pygame.K_ESCAPE:
            running = False
```

■

■

- **Mouse Input:**
  - pygame.mouse.get_pos():
    Returns the current position of
    the mouse cursor as a tuple (x,
    y).
  - pygame.mouse.get_pressed():
    Returns a tuple of boolean
    values representing the state of
    the mouse buttons (left, middle,
    right).
  - Example:
  - Python

```
mouse_x,          mouse_y          =
pygame.mouse.get_pos()
mouse_buttons                        =
pygame.mouse.get_pressed()
if mouse_buttons[0]:  # Left mouse button
    # Perform action at mouse position
    # ...
```

- ○
- ○
- ○ **Mouse Events:**
  - ■ pygame.MOUSEBUTTON DOWN: Triggered when a mouse button is pressed.
  - ■ pygame.MOUSEBUTTON UP: Triggered when a mouse button is released.
  - ■ pygame.MOUSEMOTION: Triggered when the mouse cursor moves.
  - ■ These events provide detailed information about mouse interactions.
- ● **Event Queue:**
  - ○ pygame.event.get() retrieves events from the event queue.
  - ○ It's essential to process the event queue in your game loop to prevent the game from becoming unresponsive.

3.4 Working with Sprites and Images

Sprites are the visual building blocks of 2D games. Pygame provides tools for loading, manipulating, and displaying images.[1]

- **Loading Images:**
    - pygame.image.load(filename): Loads an image from a file (e.g., PNG, JPG).
    - surface.convert(): Converts the image to the display's pixel format for optimal performance.
    - Example:
    - Python

```
player_image                    =
pygame.image.load("player.png").convert_a
lpha()
```

- $\circ$
- $\circ$
- $\circ$ .convert_alpha() is used for images with transparency.
- **Sprites:**
  - $\circ$ pygame.sprite.Sprite: A base class for creating game objects with visual representations.
  - $\circ$ You can create custom sprite classes that inherit from pygame.sprite.Sprite.
  - $\circ$ Essential sprite attributes:
    - ■ image: The sprite's image surface.
    - ■ rect: The sprite's rectangular bounding box.
  - $\circ$ Example:
  - $\circ$ Python

```
class Player(pygame.sprite.Sprite):
    def __init__(self):
        super().__init__()
```

```python
        self.image =
pygame.image.load("player.png").convert_a
lpha()
    self.rect = self.image.get_rect()
    self.rect.center = (400, 300)
```

- ○
- ○

- **Sprite Groups:**
    - ○ pygame.sprite.Group: A container for managing multiple sprites.
    - ○ Provides methods for updating, drawing, and checking collisions between sprites.
    - ○ Example:
    - ○ Python

```python
all_sprites = pygame.sprite.Group()
player = Player()
```

```
all_sprites.add(player)
all_sprites.update()
all_sprites.draw(screen)
```

- ○
- ○

- **Sprite Sheets and Animation:**
  - ○ Sprite sheets contain multiple animation frames in a single image.[2]
  - ○ You can extract individual frames using slicing techniques.
  - ○ Use a timer to cycle through animation frames.
  - ○ This is essential for creating smooth character animations.
- **Image Transformations:**
  - ○ pygame.transform.scale(surface, (width, height)): Resizes an image.
  - ○ pygame.transform.rotate(surface, angle): Rotates an image.

- pygame.transform.flip(surface, xbool, ybool): Flips an image horizontally or vertically.

3.5 Basic Game Logic and Event Handling

Game logic defines the rules and behavior of your game. Event handling allows your game to respond to user actions and system events.

- **Game Logic:**
    - Updating game variables (e.g., player position, score).
    - Implementing game rules (e.g., collision detection, scoring).
    - Managing game states (e.g., menu, gameplay, game over).
- **Event Handling:**
    - pygame.event.get(): Retrieves events from the event queue.
    - Handling events like:

- pygame.QUIT: Window close event.
- pygame.KEYDOWN, pygame.KEYUP: Keyboard input events.
- pygame.MOUSEBUTTON DOWN, pygame.MOUSEBUTTON UP, pygame.MOUSEMOTION: Mouse input events.
- pygame.USEREVENT: Custom events.
  - Example:
  - Python

```
for event in pygame.event.get():
    if event.type == pygame.QUIT:
        running = False
    elif event.type == pygame.KEYDOWN:
        if event.key == pygame.K_SPACE:
            # Perform jump action
```

- o
- o
- **Collision Detection:**
  - o pygame.sprite.collide_rect(sprite1, sprite2): Checks for rectangle collisions.
  - o pygame.sprite.collide_circle(sprite1, sprite2): Checks for circle collisions.
  - o pygame.sprite.spritecollide(sprite, group, dokill): Checks for collisions between a sprite and a sprite group.
- **Game States:**
  - o Use variables or enums to represent different game states.
  - o Switch between game states based on user input or game events.

3.6 Creating a Simple Game Example (e.g., a simple pong game)

Let's illustrate these concepts with a basic Pong game.

- **Game Elements:**
  - Player paddle.
  - Computer paddle.
  - Ball.
- **Game Logic:**
  - Ball movement.
  - Paddle movement.
  - Collision detection (ball-paddle, ball-walls).
  - Scoring.
- **Implementation:**
  - Create sprite classes for the paddles and the ball.
  - Implement movement logic for the paddles and the ball.
  - Handle collisions between the ball and the paddles and walls.

- Implement scoring logic.
- Draw the game elements on the screen.
- Control the game loop and frame rate.

By working through a simple game example like Pong, you'll gain practical experience with Pygame's features and solidify your understanding of game development concepts.

CHAPTER 4

Advanced 2D Game Mechanics and Features in Pygame

To create compelling 2D games in Pygame, developers must move beyond basic rendering and input. Key advancements include robust **collision detection** (rect, circle, pixel-perfect), immersive **sound and music integration**, and dynamic **animation techniques** using sprite sheets. These features enable more complex interactions, richer environments, and engaging gameplay.

4.1 Implementing Collision Detection

Collision detection is fundamental for creating interactive and responsive games.[1]

Pygame provides various methods for detecting collisions between game objects.[2]

- **Rectangle   Collision (pygame.Rect.colliderect())**:
    - The most basic and efficient collision detection method.
    - Checks if two rectangles intersect.
    - Useful for simple collisions between rectangular objects.
    - Example:
    - Python

```
if player_rect.colliderect(enemy_rect):
    # Collision occurred
    # ...
```

    -
    -

- **Point   Collision**
  (pygame.Rect.collidepoint()):
    - Checks if a point lies within a rectangle.
    - Useful for detecting mouse clicks on game objects or checking if a projectile hits a specific point.
    - Example:
    - Python

```
if        enemy_rect.collidepoint(mouse_x,
mouse_y):
   # Mouse click on enemy
   # ...
```

    -
    -

- **Circle   Collision**
  (pygame.sprite.collide_circle()):[3]
    - Check if two circles intersect.

- Useful for collisions between circular objects or objects with circular hitboxes.
- Requires sprites with a radius attribute.
- Example:
- Python

```
if
pygame.sprite.collide_circle(player_sprite,
enemy_sprite):
    # Collision occurred
    # ...
```

-
-
-
- **Pixel-Perfect Collision (pygame.mask.from_surface()):**

- Checks for collisions based on the actual pixels of the images.
- Useful for objects with irregular shapes or transparency.
- Creates masks from image surfaces using pygame.mask.from_surface().
- Checks for overlapping pixels using pygame.sprite.collide_mask().
- Example:
- Python

```
player_mask = pygame.mask.from_surface(player_sprite.image)
enemy_mask = pygame.mask.from_surface(enemy_sprite.image)
if pygame.sprite.collide_mask(player_sprite, enemy_sprite):
```

```
# Pixel-perfect collision occurred
# ...
```

- ○
- ○

- **Sprite Group Collisions (pygame.sprite.spritecollide()):**
  - ○ Checks for collisions between a sprite and a sprite group.[4]
  - ○ Returns a list of sprites that collide with the specified sprite.
  - ○ dokill parameter removes colliding sprites from the group.
  - ○ Example:
  - ○ Python

```
collisions =
pygame.sprite.spritecollide(player_sprite,
enemy_group, False)
for enemy in collisions:
```

```
# Handle collision with each enemy
# ...
```

- ○
- ○

- **Implementing Physics:**
  - ○ For more complex games, consider implementing basic physics:
    - Velocity and acceleration.
    - Gravity.
    - Friction.
  - ○ This can add realism to your game's movement and interactions.

4.2 Adding Sound and Music

Sound and music enhance the immersion and atmosphere of your game. Pygame provides functions for loading and playing audio.[5]

- **Loading Sound Effects (pygame.mixer.Sound()):**
  - Loads a sound effect from a file (e.g., WAV, OGG).[6]
  - Can be played multiple times simultaneously.
  - Example:
  - Python

```
sound_effect                        =
pygame.mixer.Sound("explosion.wav")
```

  -
  -

- **Playing Sound Effects (sound_effect.play()):**
  - Plays the loaded sound effect.

- Can specify the number of times to play the sound.
- Example:
- Python

```
sound_effect.play()
```

-
-

- **Loading   Music (pygame.mixer.music.load())**:
  - Loads a music file (e.g., MP3, OGG).
  - Designed for background music that plays continuously.
  - Example:
  - Python

```
pygame.mixer.music.load("background.mp3
")
```

    ○

    ○

- **Playing   Music (pygame.mixer.music.play())**:
  - Starts playing the loaded music.
  - Can specify the number of times to repeat the music.
  - Example:
  - Python

```
pygame.mixer.music.play(-1)  # -1 means
infinite loop
```

    ○

    ○

- **Controlling   Music**
  (pygame.mixer.music.pause(),
  pygame.mixer.music.unpause(),
  pygame.mixer.music.stop()**):**
  - Provides functions for pausing,
    unpausing, and stopping the
    music.
  - Example:
  - Python

```
pygame.mixer.music.pause()
pygame.mixer.music.unpause()
pygame.mixer.music.stop()
```

  -
  -

- **Volume   Control**
  (pygame.mixer.Sound.set_volume(),
  pygame.mixer.music.set_volume()**):**

- Adjusts the volume of sound effects and music.
- Takes a value between 0.0 (silent) and 1.0 (full volume).
- Example:
- Python

```
sound_effect.set_volume(0.5)
pygame.mixer.music.set_volume(0.8)
```

-
-

- **Sound Channels:**
  - Pygame's mixer can play multiple sounds simultaneously using channels.
  - You can control the volume and other properties of each channel.[7]

4.3 Animation Techniques and Sprite Sheets

Animation brings your game characters and objects to life. Pygame provides tools for creating animations using sprite sheets.[8]

- **Sprite Sheets:**
  - A single image file containing multiple animation frames.
  - Optimizes memory usage and reduces file loading times.
  - Requires slicing techniques to extract individual frames.
- **Extracting Frames:**
  - Calculate the position and size of each frame in the sprite sheet.
  - Use surface.subsurface() to extract individual frames.
  - Example:
  - Python

```
frame_width = 32
frame_height = 32
frame_rect       =       pygame.Rect(frame_x,
frame_y, frame_width, frame_height)
frame_image                              =
sprite_sheet.subsurface(frame_rect)
```

  - ○
  - ○

- **Animation Loop:**
    - ○ Use a timer to cycle through animation frames.
    - ○ Update the sprite's image with the next frame in the sequence.
    - ○ Example:
    - ○ Python

```
animation_timer += 1
if animation_timer >= animation_speed:
  animation_timer = 0
```

```
current_frame = (current_frame + 1) %
num_frames
                    player_sprite.image    =
animation_frames[current_frame]
```

- o
- o

- **Animation States:**
    - o Use different animation sequences for different character actions (e.g., walking, jumping, attacking).
    - o Switch between animation states based on player input or game events.
- **Flipping and Rotating Sprites:**
    - o pygame.transform.flip(): Flips a sprite horizontally or vertically.
    - o pygame.transform.rotate(): Rotates a sprite.
    - o Useful for creating mirrored animations or rotating objects.

- **Animation Optimization:**
  - Use sprite sheets to reduce the number of image files.[9]
  - Use optimized image formats (e.g., PNG with compression).
  - Limit the number of animation frames to improve performance.

By mastering these advanced 2D game mechanics and features, you can create more engaging and polished Pygame games.

4.4 Implementing Game States and Menus

Game states and menus are essential for creating structured and user-friendly games. They allow you to organize your game's flow and provide players with options and information.

- **Game States:**

- Game states represent different modes or phases of your game (e.g., main menu, gameplay, pause menu, game over).
- Using game states helps to organize your code and manage the game's flow.
- **Implementing Game States:**
  - Use variables or enums to represent different game states.
  - Create functions or classes for each game state to encapsulate its logic and rendering.
  - Switch between game states based on user input or game events.
  - Example:
  - Python

```python
GAME_STATE_MENU = 0
GAME_STATE_PLAYING = 1
GAME_STATE_PAUSE = 2
GAME_STATE_GAME_OVER = 3

current_state = GAME_STATE_MENU

def handle_menu_state():
    # Menu logic and rendering
    # ...
    if player_clicks_start:
        global current_state
                        current_state   =
GAME_STATE_PLAYING

def handle_playing_state():
    # Gameplay logic and rendering
    # ...
    if player_dies:
        global current_state
                        current_state   =
GAME_STATE_GAME_OVER

# In the game loop:
```

```
if current_state == GAME_STATE_MENU:
  handle_menu_state()
elif          current_state          ==
GAME_STATE_PLAYING:
  handle_playing_state()
# ...
```

- **Menus:**
  - ○ Menus provide players with options and information.
  - ○ Common menu elements include:
    - ■ Buttons.
    - ■ Text labels.
    - ■ Input fields.
  - ○ **Implementing Menus:**
    - ■ Create classes for menu elements (e.g., Button, Label).

- Use sprite groups to manage menu elements.
- Handle mouse clicks and keyboard input to interact with menu elements.
- Example:
- Python

```python
class Button(pygame.sprite.Sprite):
    def __init__(self, text, x, y):
        super().__init__()
        self.image = font.render(text, True, (255, 255, 255))
        self.rect = self.image.get_rect()
        self.rect.center = (x, y)

    def is_clicked(self, mouse_pos):
        return self.rect.collidepoint(mouse_pos)
```

- **Transitions:**
  - Smooth transitions between game states and menus enhance the user experience.
  - Implement animations or visual effects during transitions.

4.5 Working with Text and Fonts

Text and fonts are essential for displaying information, creating menus, and adding dialogue to your game. Pygame provides functions for rendering text and working with fonts.

- **Loading** **Fonts** (pygame.font.Font()):
  - Loads a font from a file (e.g., TTF) or system font.
  - Example:
  - Python

```
font = pygame.font.Font("font.ttf", 32)
```

-
-
- None as a filename will load the default system font.
- **Rendering Text (font.render()):**
  - Renders text onto a surface.
  - Takes arguments for the text string, antialiasing, and color.
  - Example:
  - Python

```
text_surface      =      font.render("Hello,
Pygame!", True, (255, 255, 255))
```

-
-

- **Drawing Text (**screen.blit()**):**
  - Draws the rendered text surface onto the screen.
  - Example:
  - Python

```
screen.blit(text_surface, (100, 100))
```

  - ○
  - ○
- **Font Attributes:**
  - font.size(text): Returns the size of the rendered text.
  - font.get_height(): Returns the height of the font.
  - font.get_linesize(): Returns the line spacing of the font.
- **Text Formatting:**
  - Use string formatting to create dynamic text.

- Implement text wrapping for long text strings.
  - Consider using text boxes or text areas for larger amounts of text.
- **Text Effects:**
  - Add effects like shadows, outlines, or gradients to text.
  - Use different fonts and styles to create visually appealing text.

4.6　Optimization and Performance Considerations

Optimization is crucial for creating smooth and responsive games, especially on less powerful hardware.

- **Frame Rate Control:**
  - Use pygame.time.Clock().tick() to limit the frame rate.
  - This prevents the game from running too fast or too slow on different computers.

- **Sprite Optimization:**
  - Use sprite sheets to reduce the number of image files.
  - Use optimized image formats (e.g., PNG with compression).
  - Minimize the size of sprite images.
  - Use sprite groups for efficient rendering and collision detection.
- **Surface Optimization:**
  - Convert surfaces to the display's pixel format using surface.convert() or surface.convert_alpha().
  - Avoid creating and destroying surfaces frequently.
  - Use pygame.display.flip() or pygame.display.update() efficiently.
- **Collision Optimization:**
  - Use efficient collision detection algorithms (e.g., rectangle collision).

- Minimize the number of collision checks.
- Use spatial partitioning techniques (e.g., quadtrees) for large numbers of objects.

- **Code Optimization:**
  - Profile your code to identify performance bottlenecks.
  - Use efficient data structures and algorithms.
  - Minimize the number of function calls and loops.
  - Consider using Cython or PyPy for performance-critical sections.

- **Resource Management:**
  - Load resources (images, sounds, fonts) only when needed.
  - Release resources when they are no longer needed.
  - Avoid memory leaks.

- **Hardware Acceleration:**
  - Enable hardware acceleration if available.

- Use OpenGL or DirectX for hardware-accelerated rendering.
- **Profiling:**
  - Use profiling tools to identify performance bottlenecks.
  - Analyze the results to optimize your code.
  - cProfile is a useful python profiler.

By implementing game states, menus, working with text and fonts, and optimizing your game's performance, you can create more polished and engaging Pygame games.

CHAPTER 5

Building a Complete 2D Game Project with Pygame

Creating a full 2D Pygame game involves several critical phases:

- **Planning and Design:** Defining the concept, mechanics, and visual style.
- **Core Mechanics Development:** Implementing player controls, collisions, and game logic.
- **Asset Creation:** Designing levels, sprites, sounds, and UI elements.
- **UI Implementation:** Building interactive menus and informative displays.
- **Testing and Polishing:** Debugging, optimizing, and refining the game.
- **Distribution:** Packaging and deploying the game for others to play.

Each stage is crucial for producing a polished, engaging, and distributable 2D game using Pygame.

5.1 Project Planning and Design

Before diving into coding, a well-defined plan and design are crucial for a successful game development project.

- **Game Concept and Genre:**
  - Clearly define the game's concept, genre (e.g., platformer, puzzle, shooter), and target audience.
  - This provides a clear vision and guides development decisions.
- **Game Mechanics and Features:**
  - Outline the core gameplay mechanics, such as player movement, combat, and interactions.

- List the essential features, such as levels, scoring, and power-ups.
- **Story and Narrative (If Applicable):**
  - Develop a compelling story or narrative to engage players.
  - Create characters, settings, and plot points.
- **Visual Style and Art Direction:**
  - Determine the game's visual style (e.g., pixel art, cartoon, realistic).
  - Create a style guide for consistency in art assets.
- **Sound and Music Design:**
  - Plan the sound effects and background music to enhance the game's atmosphere.
  - Consider the mood and tone of the game.
- **Technical Design:**
  - Choose the appropriate Pygame modules and libraries.

- Plan the game's architecture and code structure.
- Consider performance optimization and scalability.

- **Project Scope and Timeline:**
  - Define the scope of the project and set realistic goals.
  - Create a timeline with milestones to track progress.
  - Break the project into smaller, manageable tasks.
- **Prototyping:**
  - Create a simple prototype to test core gameplay mechanics.
  - This helps to identify potential issues and refine the design.
- **Documentation:**
  - Document the game's design, mechanics, and code.
  - This helps with communication and collaboration.

5.2 Developing Core Game Mechanics

Core game mechanics are the fundamental rules and interactions that define the gameplay experience.[1]

- **Player Movement and Controls:**
    - Implement smooth and responsive player movement using keyboard or mouse input.
    - Consider different movement types, such as walking, running, jumping, and flying.
    - Fine-tune the controls for optimal player experience.
- **Collision Detection and Physics:**
    - Implement accurate collision detection to handle interactions between game objects.
    - Consider adding basic physics, such as gravity, friction, and velocity.

- Use appropriate collision detection methods (e.g., rectangle, circle, pixel-perfect).
- **Combat and Interactions:**
  - Implement combat mechanics, such as attacking, shooting, and dodging.
  - Create interactions between game objects, such as picking up items and activating switches.
  - Balance the combat system.
- **Scoring and Progression:**
  - Implement a scoring system to track player progress.
  - Design a progression system with increasing difficulty and rewards.
  - Consider adding checkpoints and save points.
- **AI (If Applicable):**
  - Implement basic AI for enemies and non-player characters (NPCs).

- Consider AI behaviors, such as pathfinding, attacking, and fleeing.
- Adjust AI difficulty.

- **Game States and Menus:**
  - Implement game states, such as main menu, gameplay, pause menu, and game over.
  - Create menus for navigation, settings, and information.
  - Ensure smooth transitions between states.

- **User Interface (UI):**
  - Design a clear and intuitive UI to display information and provide feedback.
  - Consider using UI elements, such as health bars, score displays, and inventory.
  - Keep the UI uncluttered.

- **Game Logic and Event Handling:**
  - Implement game logic to manage game rules and behaviors.

- Handle events, such as player input, collisions, and timers.
- Organize game logic for clarity.

5.3 Creating Levels and Game Assets

Levels and game assets are essential for creating an immersive and engaging game world.

- **Level Design:**
  - Design levels that are challenging, engaging, and visually appealing.
  - Consider the layout, obstacles, and rewards of each level.
  - Use level editors or tile-based systems to create levels.
- **Game Assets:**
  - **Sprites:**

- Create sprites for characters, enemies, items, and environments.
- Use sprite sheets for animation.
- Consider different sprite sizes and styles.

- **Backgrounds:**
  - Create backgrounds that set the scene and enhance the game's atmosphere.
  - Consider using parallax scrolling for depth.

- **Tilesets:**
  - Create tilesets for tile-based level design.
  - Design tiles that are consistent and visually appealing.

- **Sound Effects and Music:**
  - Create or source sound effects and background music.

- Consider the mood and tone of the game.
        - Use appropriate audio formats (e.g., WAV, OGG).
    - **Fonts:**
        - Choose fonts that are readable and visually appealing.
        - Consider different font sizes and styles.
- **Asset Management:**
    - Organize game assets in a structured manner.
    - Use version control to track changes to assets.
    - Optimize assets for performance.
- **Level Loading and Management:**
    - Implement a system for loading and managing levels.
    - Consider using data files or level editors.
    - Ensure efficient loading to minimize delays.

- **Art Tools:**
  - Use programs like Aseprite, or photoshop to create your art assets.
  - Use programs like LMMS, or Bosca Ceoil to create sound assets.
- **Sound tools:**
  - Use programs such as Audacity, or Bfxr to manage and create sound effects.

By following these guidelines, you can create a complete and engaging 2D game project with Pygame. Remember to iterate, test, and refine your game throughout the development process.

5.4 Implementing User Interface (UI) Elements

A well-designed User Interface (UI) is crucial for providing players with information, feedback, and control. It enhances the overall gaming experience by making the game intuitive and engaging.

- **UI Design Principles:**
  - **Clarity and Simplicity:** UI elements should be easy to understand and use. Avoid clutter and unnecessary complexity.
  - **Consistency:** Maintain a consistent visual style and layout throughout the UI.
  - **Feedback:** Provide clear feedback to player actions (e.g., button clicks, hover effects).[1]

- ○ **Accessibility:** Consider players with disabilities and ensure the UI is accessible.
- ○ **Visual Hierarchy:** Use visual cues (e.g., size, color, contrast) to guide the player's attention.
- **UI Elements:**
  - ○ **Buttons:**
    - Interactive elements for triggering actions.
    - Implement button states (normal, hover, pressed).
    - Provide visual feedback when buttons are clicked or hovered.
  - ○ **Labels:**
    - Display text information, such as scores, health, and messages.[2]
    - Use appropriate fonts and colors.
    - Implement text wrapping for long text strings.
  - ○ **Progress Bars:**

- Display progress or status information (e.g., health, experience).[3]
- Use visual cues to indicate progress.
- **Input Fields:**
  - Allow players to enter text input (e.g., player names, passwords).
  - Implement input validation and error handling.
- **Menus:**
  - Provide navigation and options.
  - Use buttons, labels, and other UI elements to create menus.
- **Inventory and Item Displays:**
  - Display player inventory and item information.
  - Use icons and tooltips to provide details.

- **Tooltips:**
  - Provide additional information when the mouse hovers over UI elements.
- **Dialog Boxes:**
  - Display messages or prompts.
  - Implement buttons for user interaction.
- **Implementing UI Elements in Pygame:**
  - **Sprite Groups:**
    - Use sprite groups to manage UI elements efficiently.
    - Draw UI elements in the correct order to ensure they appear on top of other game elements.
  - **Rectangles and Surfaces:**
    - Use pygame.Rect and pygame.Surface to create UI elements.

- Draw shapes, images, and text onto surfaces.
  - **Event Handling:**
    - Handle mouse clicks and keyboard input to interact with UI elements.
    - Use pygame.mouse.get_pos() and pygame.mouse.get_pressed() to detect mouse interactions.
    - Use pygame.key.get_pressed() and pygame.event.get() to handle keyboard input.
  - **Fonts:**
    - Use pygame.font.Font to load and render text.
    - Choose fonts that are readable and visually appealing.
  - **Custom UI Classes:**

- Create custom UI classes that inherit from pygame.sprite.Sprite.
  - Encapsulate UI logic and rendering within classes.
- **UI Layout:**
  - Use layout managers or grid systems to organize UI elements.
  - Ensure that the UI is responsive and adapts to different screen sizes.
- **UI Libraries:**
  - Consider using UI libraries like pygame-gui to simplify UI development.

5.5 Testing, Debugging, and Polishing Your Game

Testing, debugging, and polishing are essential for creating a high-quality game.

- **Testing:**

- Unit Testing:
  - Test individual functions and classes to ensure they work correctly.
  - Use unit testing frameworks like unittest.
- Integration Testing:
  - Test the interactions between different game components.
  - Ensure that the game logic and UI work together seamlessly.
- Playtesting:
  - Have other people play your game and provide feedback.
  - Observe player behavior and identify areas for improvement.
  - Test on a variety of hardware.
- **Debugging:**
  - **Print Statements:**

- Use print() statements to inspect variable values and trace the flow of execution.
    - **Debugging Tools (IDEs):**
        - Use debugging tools in your IDE to step through code, set breakpoints, and inspect variables.
    - **Logging:**
        - Use the logging module to record errors and events.
        - Log errors to a file for later analysis.
    - **Error Handling:**
        - Implement robust error handling to prevent crashes.
        - Use try-except blocks to catch and handle exceptions.
- **Polishing:**
    - **Visual Polish:**
        - Refine the game's visuals, including sprites,

backgrounds, and UI elements.

- Ensure that the game's visual style is consistent and appealing.
- Add particle effects, animations, and visual effects to enhance the game's atmosphere.

- **Sound Polish:**
  - Refine the game's sound effects and music.
  - Ensure that the sound design is consistent and enhances the gameplay.
  - Adjust the volume and balance of sound effects and music.

- **Gameplay Polish:**
  - Fine-tune the game's mechanics and controls.
  - Balance the game's difficulty and progression.
  - Add polish to game feel.

- **Performance Optimization:**
  - Optimize the game's performance to ensure smooth gameplay.
  - Profile your code to identify performance bottlenecks.
  - Use efficient algorithms and data structures.
  - Optimize assets.
- **User Feedback:**
  - Incorporate feedback from playtesters.
  - Make adjustments based on user feedback.

5.6 Distributing Your Pygame Application

Distributing your Pygame application allows others to play your game.

- **Packaging Your Game:**

- **PyInstaller:**
    - A popular tool for creating standalone executables from Python applications.[4]
    - Creates a single executable file that includes all necessary dependencies.
    - Supports Windows, macOS, and Linux.
    - Example: `pyinstaller --onefile your_game.py`
- **cx_Freeze:**
    - Another tool for creating standalone executables.
    - Similar to PyInstaller.
- **Zip Files:**
    - Package your game files (code, assets) into a zip file.
    - Require players to have Python and Pygame installed.
- **Creating Installers:**
    - **Inno Setup (Windows):**

- A free installer creator for Windows.
- Creates professional-looking installers.
  - **DMG Canvas (macOS):**
    - A tool for creating DMG installers for macOS.
- **Distributing Your Game:**
  - **Game Platforms:**
    - Distribute your game on platforms like Steam, Itch.io, or GameJolt.[5]
    - These platforms provide distribution, marketing, and community features.
  - **Websites:**
    - Host your game on your own website or a file-sharing service.
  - **Mobile Platforms (If Applicable):**

- Use tools like Kivy or BeeWare to create mobile versions of your game.[6]
- **Documentation and Support:**
  - Provide clear instructions on how to install and play your game.
  - Create a website or forum for support.
  - Provide contact information for bug reports and feedback.
- **Legal Considerations:**
  - Obtain necessary licenses for assets (images, sounds, fonts).
  - Consider copyright and trademark issues.
  - Create a privacy policy if your game collects user data.

By implementing UI elements, thoroughly testing and polishing your game, and effectively distributing it, you can create a complete and successful Pygame project.

Part III:

Streamlining 2D Development with Arcade

CHAPTER 6

Introduction to Arcade: Modern 2D Game Development

Pygame, while a powerful and versatile tool, can sometimes feel low-level and require significant boilerplate code for common tasks. As 2D game development evolved, there was a need for a more streamlined and modern framework that could leverage Pygame's strengths while simplifying the development process. This is where Arcade comes in.

Arcade is a Python library specifically designed for creating 2D games with a focus on ease of use, modern features, and performance.[1] It builds upon Pygame, providing a higher-level API that simplifies common game development tasks, allowing developers to focus more on game design and less on low-level implementation details.

6.1 Arcade Framework Overview and Advantages

Arcade's design philosophy centers around providing a more intuitive and efficient way to create 2D games. Here's a detailed look at its overview and advantages:

- **Modern API and Design:**
  - Arcade adopts a modern, object-oriented approach, making code more organized and maintainable.
  - It provides a clear and consistent API, reducing the learning curve for developers familiar with Python.
  - It implements a Scene management system, greatly improving the organization of complex games.

- **Simplified Sprite Management:**
  - Arcade simplifies sprite creation, management, and animation.[2]
  - It provides classes for creating and managing sprites, sprite lists, and sprite sheets.[3]
  - It handles sprite batching automatically, improving rendering performance.
- **Built-in Physics Engine:**
  - Arcade includes a built-in physics engine based on Chipmunk2D.
  - This simplifies the implementation of realistic physics interactions, such as collisions, gravity, and forces.
  - It handles collision detection and response automatically, reducing the need for manual implementation.
- **Tile-Based Map Support:**

- Arcade provides built-in support for Tiled maps, a popular tile-based map editor.
- This simplifies the creation of complex and detailed game levels.
- It handles map loading, rendering, and collision detection automatically.

- **Audio and Input Handling:**
  - Arcade provides simple and intuitive functions for loading and playing audio.
  - It handles keyboard, mouse, and gamepad input efficiently.
  - It implements easy ways to manage GUI elements.

- **Performance Optimization:**
  - Arcade is designed for performance, leveraging Pygame's capabilities while adding optimizations.

- It uses sprite batching and other techniques to improve rendering speed.[4]
- It is designed to be efficient.

- **Cross-Platform Compatibility:**
  - Like Pygame, Arcade is cross-platform, supporting Windows, macOS, and Linux.
  - This allows developers to create games that can be played on multiple platforms.[5]

- **Active Community and Documentation:**
  - Arcade has an active community and comprehensive documentation.
  - This provides developers with resources and support for learning and troubleshooting.
  - The community is constantly working to improve the library.

- **Ease of Learning and Use:**

- Arcade reduces boilerplate code, allowing developers to focus on creative aspects.
- It is designed to be easy to learn, especially for those with Python and basic game development knowledge.

6.2 Setting Up and Using Arcade

To start developing games with Arcade, you need to set up your development environment and familiarize yourself with its basic usage.

- **Installation:**
  - Install Arcade using pip: pip install arcade
  - Ensure that you have Python and pip installed.
- **Creating a Basic Arcade Window:**
  - Import the arcade module.

- Create a subclass of arcade.Window.
- Override the on_draw() method to render graphics.
- Run the game loop using arcade.run().
- Example:
- Python

```python
import arcade

class MyGame(arcade.Window):
    def __init__(self, width, height, title):
        super().__init__(width, height, title)

arcade.set_background_color(arcade.color.
AMAZON)

    def on_draw(self):
        arcade.start_render()
        arcade.draw_circle_filled(400, 300, 50,
arcade.color.RED)
```

```
def main():
    window = MyGame(800, 600, "My
Arcade Game")
    arcade.run()

if __name__ == "__main__":
    main()
```

- o
- o

- **Sprite Management:**
  - o Create sprite objects using arcade.Sprite.
  - o Load images for sprites using arcade.load_texture().
  - o Create sprite lists using arcade.SpriteList.
  - o Draw sprites using sprite_list.draw().
- **Input Handling:**
  - o Override the on_key_press(), on_key_release(), and

on_mouse_motion() methods to handle input.

- Use arcade.key constants to identify keys.
- Use arcade.get_mouse_position() to get mouse position.

- **Physics Engine:**
  - Create a physics engine using arcade.PhysicsEngineSimple.
  - Add sprites to the physics engine.
  - Update the physics engine using physics_engine.update().

- **Tile Maps:**
  - Load Tiled maps using arcade.load_tilemap().
  - Create sprite lists from map layers.
  - Draw map layers using sprite_list.draw().

- **Audio:**
  - Load sounds using arcade.load_sound()

- Play sounds using sound.play()
- **Scene Management:**
  - Create scenes using arcade.Scene()
  - Add sprite lists to the scene.
  - Switch between scenes to control game states.

By mastering these fundamental aspects of Arcade, you can leverage its power and simplicity to create modern and engaging 2D games.

6.3 Arcade's Structure and Game Window Management

Arcade's architecture is designed to simplify game development by providing a structured and organized approach. Understanding its core structure and window management is essential for building robust games.

- **Arcade's Core Structure:**
  - Arcade is built around the concept of a Window class, which serves as the main container for your game.
  - The Window class manages the game loop, event handling, and rendering.
  - It provides methods for handling user input, updating game logic, and drawing graphics.
  - Arcade also uses a Scene management system, which allows for better organization of the game objects.
- **Game Window Management:**
  - **Creating a Window:**
    - You create a game window by subclassing arcade.Window.
    - The constructor of the Window class takes arguments for the

window's width, height, and title.

- You can also specify display flags, such as fullscreen or resizable.

○ **The Game Loop:**

  - Arcade's game loop is managed by the arcade.run() function.

  - The game loop calls the on_update() method to update game logic and the on_draw() method to render graphics.

  - **Event Handling:**

    - Arcade provides methods for handling various events, such as keyboard input, mouse input, and window events.

    - Override the on_key_press(),

on_key_release(),
on_mouse_motion()
, and other event
handling methods to
respond to user
actions.

- Arcade processes the
event queue, making
it simpler for the
developer.

- **Rendering:**
  - The on_draw() method is
  called every frame to
  render graphics.
  - Use Arcade's drawing
  functions to draw shapes,
  images, and text.[1]
  - Arcade automatically
  manages the rendering
  pipeline.
- **Setting Background Color:**
  - The
  arcade.set_background_c
  olor() function sets the

background color of the window.

○ **Scene Management:**

- Arcade's Scene class allows you to organize your game objects into scenes.
- Scenes can represent different game states, such as the main menu, gameplay, or pause menu.
- Scenes simplify the management of complex games with multiple states.

6.4 Simplified Sprite Management and Collision Handling

Sprites are the fundamental building blocks of 2D games, and Arcade simplifies their management and collision handling.

- **Sprite Management:**
  - **Creating Sprites:**
    - Create sprite objects using arcade.Sprite.
    - Load images for sprites using arcade.load_texture().
    - Set sprite properties, such as position, scale, and rotation.[2]
  - **Sprite Lists:**
    - Create sprite lists using arcade.SpriteList.
    - Add sprites to sprite lists to manage them efficiently.
    - Sprite lists provide methods for updating, drawing, and checking collisions between sprites.[3]
  - **Sprite Sheets:**
    - Arcade simplifies the use of sprite sheets for animation.

- Use arcade.load_spritesheet() to load sprite sheets.
- Extract individual frames from sprite sheets using slicing techniques.
  - **Drawing Sprites:**
    - Draw sprites using sprite_list.draw().
    - Arcade handles sprite batching automatically, improving rendering performance.[4]
- **Collision Handling:**
  - **Rectangle Collisions:**
    - Use arcade.check_for_collision() to check for collisions between two sprites.
    - Use arcade.check_for_collision_with_list() to check for collisions between a sprite and a sprite list.

- Pixel-Perfect Collisions:
  - Arcade also supports pixel perfect collisions.
  - This allows for more accurate collision detection for irregularly shaped sprites.
- Collision Callbacks:
  - Implement collision callbacks to handle collision events.
  - This allows you to define custom actions when collisions occur.

6.5 Introduction to Arcade's Built-in Physics Engine

Arcade's built-in physics engine, based on Chipmunk2D, simplifies the implementation of realistic physics interactions.

- **Physics Engine Basics:**
  - Arcade's physics engine simulates physical interactions between game objects.[5]
  - It handles collisions, gravity, and forces.[6]
  - It provides a realistic and responsive physics simulation.
- **Creating a Physics Engine:**
  - Create a physics engine using arcade.PhysicsEngineSimple.
  - Add sprites to the physics engine.
  - Specify the collision types for sprites.
- **Updating the Physics Engine:**
  - Update the physics engine using physics_engine.update().
  - The physics engine updates the positions and velocities of sprites based on physical forces.[7]
- **Collision Handling with Physics:**

- The physics engine automatically detects and handles collisions.[8]
- You can implement collision callbacks to handle collision events.[9]
- The physics engine provides methods for applying forces and impulses to sprites.

- **Gravity and Forces:**
  - Apply gravity to sprites using the gravity_constant parameter of the physics engine.
  - Apply forces and impulses to sprites using the apply_force() and apply_impulse() methods.

- **Collision Shapes:**
  - Arcade's physics engine supports various collision shapes, such as circles and rectangles.[10]
  - This allows you to create accurate collision detection for different types of sprites.

- **Optimization:**
  - Arcade's physics engine is optimized for performance.
  - It uses efficient algorithms and data structures.
  - However, it is still important to optimize your game's physics simulation to ensure smooth gameplay.

By mastering Arcade's structure, sprite management, and physics engine, you can create modern and engaging 2D games with ease.

CHAPTER 7

Advanced Arcade Features and Game Design

Arcade provides powerful features for creating sophisticated 2D games, including:

- **Scene Management:** Enables organized game state management and smooth transitions.
- **Advanced Sprite Animation and Effects:** Facilitates complex animations and visual effects through sprite sheets, particle systems, and shaders.[1]
- **Complex Physics with Chipmunk2D:** Allows for realistic physics interactions, collision filtering, and dynamic object behavior.

These advanced capabilities empower developers to build richer, more engaging, and visually stunning 2D game experiences with Arcade.

While Arcade simplifies basic game development, its true power lies in its advanced features that enable developers to create complex and engaging 2D games. These features, including scene management, advanced sprite animation, and a robust physics engine, allow for a higher level of game design and implementation.

7.1 Leveraging Arcade's Scene Management

Arcade's scene management system is a cornerstone of its advanced features, providing a structured approach to organizing and managing different game states.

- **Understanding Scenes:**
  - A scene in Arcade represents a distinct part of the game, such as

the main menu, gameplay, or pause menu.

- o Scenes encapsulate the logic and rendering for a specific game state.
- o They provide a clear separation of concerns, making code more organized and maintainable.

- **Creating Scenes:**
  - o Create a scene by instantiating the arcade.Scene class.
  - o Add sprite lists, tile maps, and other game objects to the scene.[1]
  - o Use the add_sprite_list() and add_tilemap_layer() methods to add objects to the scene.

- **Switching Scenes:**
  - o Use the window.show_view() method to switch between scenes.
  - o This allows you to transition smoothly between different game states.
  - o Example:

○ Python

```python
import arcade

class MainMenu(arcade.View):
    def on_show_view(self):

arcade.set_background_color(arcade.color.
BLUE)

    def on_draw(self):
        arcade.start_render()
        arcade.draw_text("Main Menu", 400,
300,        arcade.color.WHITE,        32,
anchor_x="center")

        def on_mouse_press(self, _x, _y,
_button, _modifiers):
        game_view = GameView()
        self.window.show_view(game_view)

class GameView(arcade.View):
```

```python
    def on_show_view(self):

arcade.set_background_color(arcade.color.
GRAY)

    def on_draw(self):
        arcade.start_render()
            arcade.draw_text("Game View", 400,
300,            arcade.color.BLACK,          32,
anchor_x="center")

def main():
        window = arcade.Window(800, 600,
"Scene Management Example")
    main_menu_view = MainMenu()
    window.show_view(main_menu_view)
    arcade.run()

if __name__ == "__main__":
    main()
```

○

○

- **Scene Management Benefits:**
  - **Code Organization:** Scenes improve code organization by separating game logic and rendering for different states.
  - **Modularity:** Scenes promote modularity by allowing you to create reusable game states.
  - **Maintainability:** Scenes make code easier to maintain and debug.
  - **Smooth Transitions:** Scenes facilitate smooth transitions between game states.

7.2 Advanced Sprite Animation and Effects

Arcade provides advanced features for creating sophisticated sprite animations and effects, enhancing the visual appeal of your games.

- **Sprite Sheets and Animation:**
  - Arcade simplifies the use of sprite sheets for animation.
  - Use arcade.load_spritesheet() to load sprite sheets.
  - Extract individual frames from sprite sheets using slicing techniques.
  - Create animation sequences by cycling through frames.
  - Example:
  - Python

```python
import arcade

class AnimatedSprite(arcade.Sprite):
    def __init__(self, filename, scale=1):
        super().__init__()
        self.textures = arcade.load_spritesheet(filename, 32, 32, 4)
        self.current_texture = 0
```

```python
                self.texture    =
self.textures[self.current_texture]

    def update_animation(self, delta_time:
float = 1/60):
        self.current_texture += 1
            if  self.current_texture  >=
len(self.textures):
        self.current_texture = 0
                self.texture    =
self.textures[self.current_texture]

def main():
    window  =  arcade.Window(800,  600,
"Sprite Animation Example")
                        sprite      =
AnimatedSprite("sprite_sheet.png")
    sprite.center_x = 400
    sprite.center_y = 300
    sprite_list = arcade.SpriteList()
    sprite_list.append(sprite)

    @window.event
    def on_draw():
```

```
arcade.start_render()
sprite_list.draw()

@window.event
def on_update(delta_time):
    sprite.update_animation(delta_time)

arcade.run()

if __name__ == "__main__":
    main()
```

- ○
  - ○
- **Particle Effects:**
  - ○ Arcade provides particle systems for creating visual effects, such as explosions, smoke, and fire.
  - ○ Use arcade.ParticleSystem to create particle systems.
  - ○ Configure particle properties, such as size, color, and velocity.
  - ○ Example:

○ Python

```python
import arcade

def main():
    window = arcade.Window(800, 600, "Particle System Example")
    particle_system = arcade.ParticleSystem("particle.json")

    @window.event
    def on_draw():
        arcade.start_render()
        particle_system.draw()

    @window.event
    def on_update(delta_time):
        particle_system.update()

    arcade.run()

if __name__ == "__main__":
```

main()

- ○
- ○

- **Shaders:**
  - ○ Arcade supports shaders for creating advanced visual effects.[2]
  - ○ Use shaders to create effects, such as lighting, shadows, and distortions.[3]
  - ○ Shaders provide a high level of control over rendering.[4]
- **Effects Libraries:**
  - ○ Arcade can be used with libraries that provide special effects.
  - ○ This allows for a great deal of visual control.

7.3 Creating Complex Game Mechanics with Arcade's Physics

Arcade's built-in physics engine, based on Chipmunk2D, allows you to create complex and realistic game mechanics.

- **Advanced Physics Interactions:**
    - Arcade's physics engine supports various collision shapes, such as circles, rectangles, and polygons.
    - This allows you to create accurate collision detection for complex objects.
    - You can create joints and constraints to simulate realistic physical interactions.
- **Dynamic Physics Objects:**
    - Create dynamic physics objects that respond to forces and collisions.[5]

- Use the physics engine to simulate realistic movement and interactions.[6]
- **Collision Filtering:**
  - Use collision filtering to control which objects collide with each other.
  - This allows you to create complex collision behaviors.
- **Physics Callbacks:**
  - Implement physics callbacks to handle collision events.[7]
  - This allows you to define custom actions when collisions occur.
- **Advanced Physics Examples:**
  - Create games with realistic physics-based puzzles.
  - Simulate ragdoll physics for character animations.
  - Create games with complex vehicle physics.

By leveraging these advanced features, you can create sophisticated and engaging 2D games with Arcade.

7.4 Using Arcade's Tiled Map Support

Arcade's seamless integration with Tiled, a powerful tile map editor, empowers developers to design intricate and visually appealing game levels with ease.

- **Tiled: A Versatile Level Design Tool:**
    - Tiled is a free, open-source tile map editor that allows for the creation of 2D game levels using tiles.[1]
    - Its intuitive interface simplifies level design, allowing developers to focus on creativity rather than complex coding.[2]
    - Key features include:

- Layered map creation, enabling depth and complexity.[3]
- Object layers for placing interactive elements.[4]
- Tile properties for customizing tile behavior.
- Support for various tile sizes and map orientations.

- **Integrating Tiled Maps into Arcade:**
  - Arcade's arcade.load_tilemap() function streamlines the process of loading Tiled maps.
  - This function parses the Tiled map file (.tmx) and creates Arcade-compatible data structures.
  - The arcade.Scene.from_tilemap() function will create a scene from the tile map that can then be drawn.

- ○ **Example:**
- ○ Python

```python
import arcade

def load_my_map():
    tile_map = arcade.load_tilemap("my_level.tmx", scaling=1)
    my_scene = arcade.Scene.from_tilemap(tile_map)
    return my_scene

class MyGame(arcade.Window):
    def __init__(self, width, height, title):
        super().__init__(width, height, title)
        self.my_scene = load_my_map()

    def on_draw(self):
        arcade.start_render()
        self.my_scene.draw()
```

```
def main():
    window = MyGame(800, 600, "Tiled Map
Integration")
    arcade.run()

if __name__ == "__main__":
    main()
```

○

○

- **Leveraging Map Layers and Objects:**
  - ○ Tiled's layer system allows for the creation of foreground, background, and collision layers.[5]
  - ○ Arcade provides access to these layers as sprite lists, enabling efficient rendering and collision detection.[6]
  - ○ Object layers can be used to place interactive elements like

player spawn points, enemy locations, and collectibles.

- Object properties allow for customization of these elements, adding flexibility to level design.

- **Collision Detection with Tiled Maps:**
  - Arcade's collision detection functions can be used to check for collisions between game objects and tile map layers.[7]
  - This simplifies the implementation of platforming mechanics, obstacle avoidance, and other interactions.
  - By checking collisions against the collision layer, you can create solid platforms and walls.

7.5 Implementing Advanced UI and GUI Elements: Enhancing User Interaction

Arcade's flexibility allows for the creation of sophisticated UI and GUI elements, providing players with intuitive control and information.

- **GUI Libraries: Streamlining UI Development:**
    - Libraries like arcade-gui and arcade-ui provide pre-built UI components, such as buttons, sliders, and text inputs.
    - These libraries simplify UI development by providing layout managers, event handling, and styling options.
    - They reduce the need for manual UI element creation, saving development time.
- **Custom UI Elements: Tailored User Interfaces:**

- For unique UI designs, developers can create custom UI elements using Arcade's drawing functions and sprite capabilities.[8]
- By subclassing arcade.Sprite or arcade.View, developers can create interactive UI components with custom behavior.
- Example:
- Python

```python
import arcade

class MyButton(arcade.Sprite):
    def __init__(self, text, x, y):
        super().__init__()
        self.text = text
        self.texture = arcade.make_text_image(text,
arcade.color.WHITE, 24)
```

```
        self.center_x = x
        self.center_y = y

    def draw(self):

arcade.draw_texture_rectangle(self.center_
x,     self.center_y,     self.texture.width,
self.texture.height, self.texture)

    def is_mouse_over(self, x, y):
            return abs(x - self.center_x) <
self.texture.width  /  2  and  abs(y  -
self.center_y) < self.texture.height / 2

# Example usage within an Arcade View
```

○

○

- **Layout Management and Event Handling:**
    - ○ Layout managers, either built-in or provided by GUI libraries,

simplify the arrangement of UI elements.[9]

- ○ Event handling allows for the implementation of interactive UI components, responding to mouse clicks, keyboard input, and other events.[10]
- ○ By implementing event callbacks, developers can create dynamic UI interactions.

- **Visual Effects and Animations:**
  - ○ Adding visual effects and animations to UI elements enhances their appeal and provides feedback to user actions.
  - ○ Particle systems, shaders, and sprite animations can be used to create visually stunning UI components.

7.6 Building a Platformer Game Example using Arcade: Putting it All Together

Creating a platformer game example demonstrates the practical application of Arcade's features.

- **Game Design and Planning:**
  - Define the game's core mechanics, such as player movement, jumping, and collision detection.
  - Design levels using Tiled, incorporating platforms, obstacles, and collectibles.
  - Plan the game's UI, including health bars, score displays, and menus.
- **Implementation:**
  - Load the Tiled map and create the game scene.

- Create a player sprite and implement movement controls using keyboard input.
- Implement collision detection between the player and the tile map layers.
- Apply gravity and implement jumping mechanics.
- Add enemies and collectibles, implementing AI and interaction logic.
- Create UI elements using custom sprites or a GUI library.
- Implement game states using Arcade's scene management.
- Add sound effects and background music.
- Test, debug, and polish the game.

- **Key Techniques:**
  - Use arcade.check_for_collision_with_list() for collision detection.

- Implement physics-based movement using Arcade's physics engine.[11]
- Use sprite sheets for character animations.
- Use object layers in Tiled to place interactive game objects.
- Use scene management to create a main menu, game over screen, and other game states.

- **Example Code Snippet (Player Movement):**
- Python

```python
def on_update(self, delta_time):
    self.player_sprite.change_x = 0
    keys = arcade.key.get_pressed()
    if keys[arcade.key.LEFT]:
            self.player_sprite.change_x = -PLAYER_MOVEMENT_SPEED
    if keys[arcade.key.RIGHT]:
            self.player_sprite.change_x = PLAYER_MOVEMENT_SPEED
```

```
# Implement jumping logic here
# ...

self.physics_engine.update()
```

-
-

By building a platformer game example, developers gain hands-on experience with Arcade's advanced features, solidifying their understanding of 2D game development.

Part IV:

Transitioning to 3D with Panda3D

CHAPTER 8

Introduction to 3D Game Development and Panda3D

Moving from 2D to 3D game development introduces a new level of complexity and immersion. 3D games allow for the creation of rich, interactive environments that engage players on a deeper level.[1] Panda3D, a powerful and versatile 3D game engine, empowers developers to bring their 3D visions to life.[2]

8.1 Understanding 3D Game Development Concepts (Vertices, Polygons, Textures)

To effectively work with 3D game engines like Panda3D, it's essential to understand the fundamental concepts that underpin 3D graphics.

- **Vertices:**
  - Vertices are the basic building blocks of 3D models.[3]
  - A vertex is a point in 3D space, defined by its x, y, and z coordinates.
  - Vertices define the corners of polygons.[4]
  - They carry data such as position, color, and texture coordinates.
- **Polygons:**
  - Polygons are flat surfaces formed by connecting vertices.
  - Triangles are the most common type of polygon used in 3D graphics because they are:
    - Always planar (lie on a single plane).
    - Efficient to render.
    - Can represent any shape when combined.
  - Quads (four-sided polygons) are also used, but they can be

problematic if they are not planar.
- A mesh is a collection of polygons that form a 3D model.
- **Textures:**
  - Textures are images that are applied to the surfaces of polygons.[5]
  - They add detail and realism to 3D models.[6]
  - Textures are mapped to polygons using texture coordinates (UV coordinates).[7]
  - Texture mapping involves wrapping a 2D image onto a 3D surface.[8]
  - Different kinds of texture exist, for example:
    - Diffuse maps: defines the colors of a surface.
    - Normal maps: give a surface the appearance of fine details.[9]

- Specular maps: define how shiny a surface is.[10]
- **3D Space and Coordinate Systems:**
    - 3D space is defined by three axes: x, y, and z.[11]
    - Understanding coordinate systems is crucial for positioning and transforming objects in 3D space.[12]
    - Panda3D uses a right-handed coordinate system.[13]
- **Transformations:**
    - Transformations are used to move, rotate, and scale 3D objects.
    - These transformations are performed using matrices.
    - Understanding matrix transformations is essential for 3D game development.
- **Rendering Pipeline:**
    - The rendering pipeline is the sequence of steps that are

performed to render a 3D scene.[14]
- It involves vertex processing, rasterization, and fragment processing.
- Understanding the rendering pipeline helps to optimize 3D graphics.[15]

8.2 Panda3D Framework Overview and Architecture

Panda3D is a powerful and open-source 3D game engine developed by Disney Interactive.[16] It's known for its flexibility, extensibility, and cross-platform capabilities.

- **Key Features:**
  - **Scene Graph:** Panda3D uses a scene graph to manage 3D objects.[17]

- **Rendering Pipeline:** It provides a flexible and customizable rendering pipeline.[18]
- **Physics Engine:** It integrates with physics engines, such as Bullet and PhysX.[19]
- **Animation System:** It offers a robust animation system for character animation.
- **Networking:** It supports network multiplayer games.[20]
- **Cross-Platform:** It runs on Windows, macOS, and Linux.[21]
- **Python Integration:** It's tightly integrated with Python, making it easy to use and extend.[22]

- **Architecture:**
  - Panda3D is written in C++ for performance, with a Python interface for scripting and development.[23]

- Its architecture is designed for modularity and extensibility.[24]
- The scene graph is a core component of its architecture, providing a hierarchical structure for organizing 3D objects.
- The rendering pipeline is customizable, allowing developers to implement advanced rendering techniques.

- **Advantages:**
  - **Open-Source:** It's free to use and modify.
  - **Powerful:** It can be used to create high-quality 3D games.[25]
  - **Flexible:** It allows for a high degree of customization.
  - **Python-Friendly:** It's easy to use for Python developers.

8.3 Setting Up Panda3D and Understanding its Scene Graph

Setting up Panda3D and understanding its scene graph are the first steps in 3D game development.

- **Installation:**
  - Panda3D can be installed using installers or package managers.[26]
  - Follow the instructions on the Panda3D website for your operating system.
- **Basic Panda3D Setup:**
  - Import the Panda3D modules.
  - Create a ShowBase object, which initializes the engine.
  - Load 3D models.
  - Run the Panda3D game loop.
  - Example:
  - Python

```python
from panda3d.core import *
from direct.showcase.ShowCase import ShowBase

class MyApp(ShowBase):
    def __init__(self):
        ShowBase.__init__(self)
        self.scene = self.loader.loadModel("models/environment")
        self.scene.reparentTo(self.render)
        self.scene.setScale(0.25, 0.25, 0.25)
        self.scene.setPos(-8, 42, 0)

app = MyApp()
app.run()
```

- ○
  - ○
- **Scene Graph:**
  - ○ The scene graph is a hierarchical structure that organizes 3D objects.[27]

- Nodes are the elements of the scene graph.[28]
- Nodes can be parents or children of other nodes.[29]
- Nodes can represent 3D models, cameras, lights, and other game objects.[30]
- The scene graph provides an efficient way to manage and manipulate 3D objects.
- By reparenting a node, the child node inherits the transform information of the parent node.

- **NodePath:**
  - In Panda3D, all nodes are handled through a NodePath.[31]
  - The NodePath object provides a layer of functionality over the node.[32]
  - It enables the developer to easily transform nodes.
  - All operations such as loading a model, will return a NodePath.

By understanding these concepts, you'll be well-prepared to embark on your 3D game development journey with Panda3D.

8.4 Loading and Manipulating 3D Models

3D models are the visual heart of any 3D game. Panda3D provides robust tools for loading and manipulating these models.[1]

- **Loading 3D Models:**
    - Panda3D supports various 3D model formats, including .egg, .bam, .obj, and .fbx.
    - Use the loader.loadModel() method to load 3D models.
    - Example:
    - Python

from panda3d.core import *

```
from    direct.showcase.ShowCase    import
ShowBase

class MyApp(ShowBase):
  def __init__(self):
    ShowBase.__init__(self)
                          self.model     =
self.loader.loadModel("models/my_model.e
gg")
    self.model.reparentTo(self.render)

app = MyApp()
app.run()
```

- ○
- ○
- ○ .bam files are a compiled format
  that Panda3D can load more
  quickly than .egg files.
- **Manipulating 3D Models:**
  - ○ **Transformations:**
    - ■ Use setPos(), setHpr()
      (heading, pitch, roll), and

setScale() to transform models.

- These methods modify the model's position, rotation, and scale in 3D space.[2]
- Example:
- Python

```
self.model.setPos(0, 10, 0)
self.model.setHpr(45, 0, 0)
self.model.setScale(2, 2, 2)
```

-
-
  - **Parenting:**
    - Use reparentTo() to parent models to other nodes in the scene graph.

- This allows for hierarchical transformations and organization.
- Example:
- Python

```
self.model.reparentTo(self.render) # Parent to the render node.
```

-
-

- **NodePath Operations:**
  - NodePath objects provide a wide range of methods for manipulating models.[3]
  - Use find(), findAllMatches(), and

getChild() to navigate the scene graph.

- Use attachNewNode() to create new nodes and parent them to models.

- **Materials and Textures:**
  - Use setMaterial() and setTexture() to apply materials and textures to models.
  - Materials define the surface properties of models, such as color and shininess.[4]
  - Textures add detail and realism to models.[5]
  - Example:
  - Python

```
texture                            =
self.loader.loadTexture("textures/my_textu
re.png")
self.model.setTexture(texture)
```

■

■

- ○ **Animations:**
  - ■ Panda3D provides a robust animation system for animating models.
  - ■ Load animations using loader.loadAnims().
  - ■ Use control() and loop() to play animations.
  - ■ Example:
  - ■ Python

```python
anims    =    self.loader.loadAnims({"walk":
"models/my_model_walk.egg"})
self.model.control("walk", loop=True)
```

8.5 Basic 3D Rendering and Camera Control

Rendering and camera control are essential for creating visually appealing 3D scenes.

- **Basic Rendering:**
  - Panda3D's rendering pipeline handles the process of drawing 3D objects to the screen.[6]

- The render node is the root of the scene graph, representing the 3D world.
- Use render.attachNewNode() to create new nodes and add them to the scene.
- Panda3D will render all objects that are children of the render node.

- **Camera Control:**
  - The camera defines the viewpoint from which the 3D scene is rendered.
  - Panda3D provides a default camera, which can be accessed using base.camera.
  - Use setPos(), setHpr(), and lookAt() to control the camera.
  - Example:
  - Python

```
base.camera.setPos(0, -20, 10)
```

base.camera.lookAt(self.model)

- ○
- ○
- ○ **Camera Movement:**
  - ■ Implement camera movement using keyboard or mouse input.
  - ■ Use base.disableMouse() to disable the default mouse camera control.
  - ■ Example:
  - ■ Python

```
def update_camera(task):
                              if
base.mouseWatcherNode.isButtonDown(Ke
yboardButton.ascii_key("w")):
```

```
    base.camera.setY(base.camera.getY() +
1)
  return task.cont

taskMgr.add(update_camera,
"camera_task")
```

■
■

- ○ **Projection Matrices:**
    - ■ Panda3D uses projection matrices to transform 3D coordinates into 2D screen coordinates.[7]
    - ■ The projection matrix defines the camera's field of view and aspect ratio.
    - ■ Use base.camLens to access and modify the camera's lens.
- **Lighting and Shadows:**

- Lighting adds realism and depth to 3D scenes.[8]
- Panda3D supports various types of lights, including ambient lights, directional lights, and point lights.[9]
- Shadows enhance the realism of lighting.
- Example:
- Python

```
directionalLight                    =
DirectionalLight("directionalLight")
directionalLightNP                  =
render.attachNewNode(directionalLight)
directionalLight NP.setUp(0, -60, 0)
render.setLight(directionalLightNP)
```

-
-

8.6 Essential 3D Math for Game Development

3D game development relies heavily on mathematical concepts to create realistic and interactive environments. Key areas include:

- **Vectors:** Representing direction and magnitude for positions, velocities, and forces.
- **Matrices:** Handling linear transformations like rotation, scaling, and translation.
- **Quaternions:** Managing rotations to avoid gimbal lock and ensure smooth movement.
- **Transformations:** Combining vectors and matrices to manipulate 3D objects in space.
- **Coordinate Systems:** Understanding different coordinate systems and their conversions.

- **Linear Algebra:** Providing the theoretical basis for vector and matrix operations.

Mastering these mathematical tools is crucial for developers to effectively manipulate 3D objects, control cameras, and implement realistic physics in their games.

CHAPTER 9

Advanced 3D Game Mechanics in Panda3D

Advanced 3D game mechanics in Panda3D allow developers to create truly immersive and interactive experiences. By mastering collision detection, physics, lighting, shaders, textures, and materials, you can bring your 3D worlds to life with stunning realism and engaging gameplay.

9.1 Implementing 3D Collision Detection and Physics

Collision detection and physics are fundamental for creating realistic interactions between objects in a 3D environment.[1] Panda3D integrates with powerful physics engines to provide robust physics simulations.[2]

- **Collision Detection:**
  - **Collision Solids:** Panda3D provides various collision solids, such as CollisionSphere, CollisionBox, CollisionPolygon, and CollisionRay.
  - **Collision Nodes:** Collision solids are attached to CollisionNode objects, which are then added to the scene graph.
  - **Collision Handlers:** Use CollisionHandlerQueue and CollisionTraverser to detect and handle collisions.
  - **Example:**
  - Python

```python
from panda3d.core import *
from direct.showcase.ShowCase import ShowBase

class MyApp(ShowBase):
```

```python
def __init__(self):
    ShowBase.__init__(self)
    self.sphere = self.loader.loadModel("models/sphere")
    self.sphere.reparentTo(self.render)
    self.sphere.setPos(0, 10, 0)

    sphere_collision = CollisionSphere(0, 0, 0, 1)
    sphere_node = CollisionNode("sphere_collision")

    sphere_node.addSolid(sphere_collision)
    sphere_node_path = self.sphere.attachNewNode(sphere_node)

    self.box = self.loader.loadModel("models/box")
    self.box.reparentTo(self.render)
    self.box.setPos(0, 0, 0)

    box_collision = CollisionBox(Point3(-1, -1, -1), Point3(1, 1, 1))
```

```
                        box_node      =
CollisionNode("box_collision")
    box_node.addSolid(box_collision)
                  box_node_path      =
self.box.attachNewNode(box_node)

    self.traverser = CollisionTraverser()
    self.queue = CollisionHandlerQueue()

self.traverser.addCollider(sphere_node_pat
h, self.queue)

    def update_collisions(task):
        self.traverser.traverse(self.render)
        for entry in self.queue.getEntries():
            print("Collision!")
        self.queue.clearEntries()
        return task.cont

            taskMgr.add(update_collisions,
"collisions")

app = MyApp()
app.run()
```

- o
- o
- **Physics Engines (Bullet/PhysX):**
  - o Panda3D integrates with physics engines like Bullet and PhysX to simulate realistic physics.[3]
  - o Use BulletWorld or PhysXWorld to create a physics world.
  - o Add rigid bodies and collision shapes to the physics world.
  - o Apply forces, torques, and impulses to rigid bodies.
  - o Example (Bullet):
  - o Python

```python
from panda3d.core import *
from direct.showcase.ShowCase import ShowBase
from panda3d.bullet import *

class MyApp(ShowBase):
    def __init__(self):
```

```python
ShowBase.__init__(self)
self.world = BulletWorld()
self.world.setGravity(Vec3(0, 0, -9.81))

self.sphere = self.loader.loadModel("models/sphere")
self.sphere.reparentTo(self.render)
self.sphere.setPos(0, 10, 0)

shape = BulletSphereShape(1)
body = BulletRigidBodyNode("sphere_body")
body.addShape(shape)
body_node_path = self.sphere.attachNewNode(body)
self.world.attachRigidBody(body)

def update_physics(task):
    dt = globalClock.getDt()
    self.world.doPhysics(dt)
    return task.cont

taskMgr.add(update_physics, "physics")
```

```
app = MyApp()
app.run()
```

○

○

9.2 Working with Lighting and Shaders

Lighting and shaders are essential for creating visually stunning 3D scenes. Panda3D provides powerful tools for working with both.

- **Lighting:**
  - **Light Types:** Panda3D supports various light types, including AmbientLight, DirectionalLight, PointLight, and Spotlight.

- Light Nodes: Create light nodes and attach them to the scene graph.
- Light Attributes: Set light attributes, such as color, intensity, and attenuation.[4]
- Example:
- Python

```
directionalLight                    =
DirectionalLight("directionalLight")
directionalLight.setColor((1, 1, 1, 1))
directionalLightNP                  =
render.attachNewNode(directionalLight)
directionalLightNP.setHpr(0, -60, 0)
render.setLight(directionalLightNP)
```

- ○
- ○

- **Shaders:**

- **GLSL Shaders:** Panda3D uses GLSL (OpenGL Shading Language) shaders.[5]
- **Vertex and Fragment Shaders:** Shaders consist of vertex shaders and fragment shaders.[6]
- **Shader Attributes:** Set shader attributes, such as uniforms and attributes.
- **Shader Application:** Apply shaders to nodes using setShader().
- Example:
- Python

```python
shader = Shader.load(Shader.SL_GLSL,

vertex="shaders/my_vertex.glsl",

fragment="shaders/my_fragment.glsl")
self.model.setShader(shader)
```

○
○

9.3 Creating and Applying Textures and Materials

Textures and materials add detail and realism to 3D models.[7] Panda3D provides tools for creating and applying both.

- **Textures:**
    - **Loading Textures:** Load textures using loader.loadTexture().
    - **Texture Attributes:** Set texture attributes, such as wrap modes and filtering modes.[8]
    - **Texture Application:** Apply textures to models using setTexture().
    - Example:
    - Python

```
texture                          =
self.loader.loadTexture("textures/my_textu
re.png")
self.model.setTexture(texture)
```

- ○
- ○

- **Materials:**
  - ○ **Material Creation:** Create materials using Material().
  - ○ **Material Attributes:** Set material attributes, such as ambient, diffuse, and specular colors.
  - ○ **Material Application:** Apply materials to models using setMaterial().
  - ○ Example:
  - ○ Python

```
material = Material()
material.setAmbient((0.2, 0.2, 0.2, 1))
material.setDiffuse((0.8, 0.8, 0.8, 1))
material.setSpecular((1, 1, 1, 1))
material.setShininess(50)
self.model.setMaterial(material)
```

- o
  - o

- **Texture Mapping:**
  - Use texture coordinates (UV coordinates) to map textures to models.[9]
  - Panda3D automatically generates texture coordinates for basic shapes.[10]
  - Manually create texture coordinates for complex models.
- **Normal Maps and Specular Maps:**
  - Use normal maps to add fine details to surfaces.

- Use specular maps to control the shininess of surfaces.
- **Texture Stages:**
  - Use texture stages to apply multiple textures to a model.[11]
  - Texture stages allow for blending and combining textures.[12]

By mastering these advanced 3D game mechanics, you can create immersive and visually stunning 3D games with Panda3D.

9.4 Animating 3D Models and Characters

Animation is crucial for bringing 3D models and characters to life. Panda3D provides a robust animation system for creating realistic and engaging animations.

- **Animation Basics:**

- **Animation Files:** Panda3D supports various animation formats, including .egg, .bam, and .fbx.
- **Animation Control:** Use model.control() and model.loop() to play animations.
- **Animation Blending:** Blend animations together for smooth transitions.
- **Animation Events:** Trigger events at specific points in an animation.
- **Loading Animations:**
  - Load animations using loader.loadAnims().
  - Specify the animation name and file path.
  - Example:
  - Python

```
anims    =    self.loader.loadAnims({"walk":
"models/character_walk.egg"})
```

- o
- o

- **Playing Animations:**
  - o Use model.control(anim_name, fromFrame=None, toFrame=None) to play an animation.
  - o Use model.loop(anim_name, fromFrame=None, toFrame=None) to loop an animation.
  - o Use model.stop(anim_name) to stop an animation.
  - o Example:
  - o Python

```
self.character.control("walk", loop=True)
```

- ○
- ○
- **Animation Blending:**
  - ○ Use model.blendAnims(blend_time, anim_name1, anim_name2) to blend two animations together.
  - ○ This creates smooth transitions between animations.
  - ○ Example:
  - ○ Python

```python
self.character.blendAnims(0.5, "walk", "run")
```

- ○
- ○
- **Animation Events:**

- o Use model.setPlayRate(rate, anim_name) to control the animation playback speed.
- o Use model.getCurrentAnim() to get the currently playing animation.
- o Use model.getCurrentFrame() to get the current animation frame.
- o Use model.setFrame(frame, anim_name) to set the current animation frame.
- **Skeletal Animation:**
  - o Skeletal animation involves animating a skeleton and skinning the model to the skeleton.[1]
  - o This allows for realistic character animations.
  - o Panda3D supports skeletal animation.[2]
  - o Use Actor classes for skeletal animation.
- **Animation Trees:**

- Animation trees allow for complex animation blending and control.
- They are used to create realistic character animations.
- Panda3D supports animation trees.

9.5 Implementing 3D Audio and Sound Effects

3D audio and sound effects enhance the immersion and realism of 3D games.[3] Panda3D provides tools for working with 3D audio.[4]

- **Audio Basics:**
  - **Sound Files:** Panda3D supports various audio formats, including .wav, .ogg, and .mp3.
  - **Sound Nodes:** Create sound nodes and attach them to the scene graph.

- ○ **Sound Attributes:** Set sound attributes, such as volume, pitch, and attenuation.
- ○ **3D Sound:** Position sound nodes in 3D space to create 3D audio.
- **Loading Sounds:**
  - ○ Load sounds using loader.loadSfx().
  - ○ Specify the sound file path.
  - ○ Example:
  - ○ Python

```
sound                          =
self.loader.loadSfx("sounds/my_sound.wav
")
```

  - ○
  - ○
- **Playing Sounds:**

- Use sound.play() to play a sound.
- Use sound.stop() to stop a sound.
- Use sound.setLoop(loop) to loop a sound.
- Example:
- Python

```
self.sound.play()
```

-
-

- **3D Sound:**
  - Create sound nodes and attach them to the scene graph.
  - Set the sound node's position in 3D space.

- Use set3dAttributes() to set 3D sound attributes, such as attenuation and rolloff.
- Use setListener() to set the listener's position and orientation.
- Example:
- Python

```
sound_node = self.render.attachNewNode("sound_node")
sound_node.setPos(0, 10, 0)
sound.set3dAttributes(10, 10, 1) # Attenuation, MaxDistance, Rolloff
sound.set3dListener(base.camera)
sound.play()
```

-
-

- **Audio Channels:**

- Use audio channels to control the playback of multiple sounds.
- This allows for mixing and managing sounds.
- **Audio Effects:**
    - Use audio effects to add reverb, echo, and other effects to sounds.
    - Panda3D supports various audio effects.[5]

9.6 Creating a 3D Scene Example

Let's illustrate these concepts by creating a 3D scene example using Panda3D.

- **Scene Elements:**
    - A 3D model of a character.
    - A 3D model of a terrain.
    - A directional light.
    - A sound effect.
    - An animation.
- **Implementation:**

- Load the character model and terrain model.
- Load the animation and sound effect.
- Create a directional light and add it to the scene.
- Create a sound node and attach it to the character model.
- Play the animation and sound effect.
- Implement camera control using keyboard input.
- Implement collision detection between the character and terrain.
- Implement animation blending for smooth transitions.
- Test, debug, and polish the scene.

- **Example Code Snippet (Animation):**
- Python

```python
anims = self.loader.loadAnims({"walk":
"models/character_walk.egg", "run":
"models/character_run.egg"})
self.character =
self.loader.loadModel("models/character.eg
g")
self.character.reparentTo(self.render)
self.character.loop("walk")

def update_animation(task):
    keys = base.win.getKeyboardMap()
    if keys["shift"]:
        self.character.blendAnims(0.5, "walk",
"run")
    else:
        self.character.blendAnims(0.5, "run",
"walk")
    return task.cont

taskMgr.add(update_animation,
"animation_task")
```

-
-

By creating a 3D scene example, you'll gain practical experience with Panda3D's advanced features and solidify your understanding of 3D game development concepts.

CHAPTER 10

User Interaction and Game Logic in 3D Environments

User interaction and game logic are the dynamic forces that transform a static 3D environment into a living, breathing game. These elements are the foundation upon which player engagement, narrative, and challenge are built. Panda3D provides a rich toolset to handle complex input and manage intricate game states, allowing developers to create deeply immersive 3D experiences.[1]

10.1 Handling 3D User Input (Mouse, Keyboard, Gamepad): The Player's Voice

In a 3D environment, the player's ability to navigate, manipulate, and interact is paramount. Panda3D offers a flexible and powerful input system to capture and interpret user actions from various devices.[2]

- **Keyboard Input: Precision and Control**
  - **Direct Key State Polling:**
    - Panda3D's base.win.getKeyboardMap() provides a dictionary-like object that reflects the current state of each key.
    - This method is efficient for continuous input, such as character movement or camera rotation.
    - Example:
    - Python

```
def update_movement(task):
    keys = base.win.getKeyboardMap()
```

```
if keys.get('w'):
    # Move player forward
        player.setPos(player.getPos() +
player.getNetTransform().getMat().getRow3
(1) * delta_time * move_speed)
    if keys.get('s'):
    # Move player backward
        player.setPos(player.getPos() -
player.getNetTransform().getMat().getRow3
(1) * delta_time * move_speed)
    return task.cont
taskMgr.add(update_movement,
'movement_task')
```

- ■
- ■

- ○ **Event-Driven Input:**
  - ■ Panda3D's `base.accept()` function allows you to bind specific actions to key press or release events.

- This method is ideal for discrete actions, such as jumping, firing, or menu selection.
- Example:
- Python

```python
def jump():
    # Player jump logic
    pass
base.accept('space', jump)
```

- ■
- ■
- **Mouse Input: Precision and Interaction**
  - ○ **Mouse Position and Movement:**

- base.mouseWatcherNode. getMouse() returns the mouse cursor's normalized position within the window.
- This data can be used to control camera rotation, object selection, or UI interaction.
- Example:
- Python

```python
def update_camera_rotation(task):
    if base.mouseWatcherNode.hasMouse():
        mouse_pos = base.mouseWatcherNode.getMouse()
        camera_heading = mouse_pos.getX() * rotation_speed
        camera_pitch = mouse_pos.getY() * rotation_speed
```

```python
    base.camera.setUp(camera_heading,
-camera_pitch, 0)
    return task.cont
taskMgr.add(update_camera_rotation,
'camera_rotation_task')
```

- ■
- ■
  - ○ **Mouse Button Events:**
    - ■ base.mouseWatcherNode.i sButtonDown() checks the state of mouse buttons.
    - ■ base.accept() can bind actions to mouse button events.
    - ■ Example:
    - ■ Python

```
def handle_click():
    # Perform action on click
    pass
base.accept('mouse1', handle_click)
```

- ■
- ■
  - ○ **Raycasting for 3D Interaction:**
    - ■ Raycasting allows you to determine which 3D objects the mouse cursor is pointing at.
    - ■ This is crucial for object selection, interaction, and targeting.
    - ■ Panda3D collision traversers are used to implement raycasting.
- • **Gamepad Input: Immersive Control**
  - ○ **Gamepad Device Detection:**

- Panda3D's direct.controls.InputState module provides access to connected gamepad devices.
- InputState.getDevices() returns a list of connected gamepads.
  - **Gamepad Axis and Button Input:**
    - InputState.isSet() checks the state of gamepad buttons.
    - InputState.getValue() retrieves the values of gamepad axes.
    - Example:
    - Python

```
from direct.controls.InputState import InputState
```

```
InputState.init()
def update_gamepad_input(task):
    devices = InputState.getDevices()
    if devices:
        gamepad = devices[0]
            if  InputState.isSet('gamepad-a',
gamepad):
        # A button pressed
        pass
                                        axis_x     =
InputState.getValue('gamepad-axis-x',
gamepad)
        # Use axis_x for movement
    return task.cont
taskMgr.add(update_gamepad_input,
'gamepad_input_task')
```

■
■

- **Advanced Input Techniques:**

- **Input Smoothing:** Using interpolation or filtering to smooth out jerky input.
- **Input Buffering:** Queuing player inputs for later processing.
- **Contextual Input:** Changing input behavior based on game state.
- **Custom Input Mappings:** Allowing players to remap controls.

10.2 Implementing Game Logic and State Management in 3D: The Game's Brain

Game logic and state management are the core of a 3D game, dictating its behavior and progression. Panda3D provides a robust framework for implementing complex game logic.

- **Game Loop and Task Management:**
  - Panda3D's taskMgr allows you to schedule functions (tasks) to be executed every frame.
  - This is the heart of the game loop, where game logic, physics updates, and rendering occur.
  - Example:
  - Python

```python
def update_game_logic(task):
    # Update player position, enemy AI, etc.
    return task.cont
taskMgr.add(update_game_logic, 'game_logic_task')
```

  -
  -

- **Game State Management:**

- **Finite State Machines (FSMs):**
  - FSMs are a powerful tool for managing complex game states, such as menus, gameplay, and cutscenes.[3]
  - They define a set of states and transitions between them.
  - Example:
  - Python

```python
class GameState():
    def __init__(self, game):
        self.game = game
    def enter(self): pass
    def update(self, task): pass
    def exit(self): pass
class MenuState(GameState):
    def update(self, task):
```

```
    # Menu logic
    return task.cont
class GameplayState(GameState):
  def update(self, task):
    # Gameplay logic
    return task.cont
# State management code
```

- ■
  - ■
    - ○ **State Transitions:**
      - ■ Implement smooth transitions between game states using animations or visual effects.
    - ○ **State Data:**
      - ■ Store state-specific data, such as player scores, inventory, or level progress.
  - • **Game Logic Patterns and Architecture:**

- Entity-Component System (ECS):
    - ECS is a design pattern that separates game logic and data into entities, components, and systems.[4]
    - This promotes modularity, flexibility, and performance.
- Observer Pattern:
    - Allows game components to communicate with each other without direct dependencies.
- Command Pattern:
    - Encapsulates game actions as objects, allowing for undo/redo functionality or input queuing.
- **Game Logic Components:**
    - **Player Controller:** Manages player input and actions.
    - **AI Controller:** Handles enemy AI and behavior.

- **Physics Controller:** Manages physics interactions.
- **Animation Controller:** Manages character animations.[5]
- **UI Controller:** Manages user interface elements.
- **Game Logic Communication:**
  - **Events and Messages:** Use events or messages to communicate between game components, promoting decoupling.
  - **Message Queues:** Implement message queues for asynchronous communication.
- **Game Logic Testing and Optimization:**
  - **Unit Testing:** Write unit tests to verify the correctness of game logic.
  - **Profiling:** Use profiling tools to identify performance bottlenecks.

- o **Optimization Techniques:** Employ efficient algorithms and data structures.
- **Game Logic Design Principles:**
  - o **Modularity:** Break down game logic into reusable components.
  - o **Maintainability:** Write clean, well-documented code.
  - o **Extensibility:** Design game logic that can be easily extended with new features.

By mastering these techniques, developers can create complex, engaging, and dynamic 3D game experiences with Panda3D.

10.3 Creating Interactive 3D Environments

Interactive 3D environments are the soul of engaging games. They allow players to feel immersed and connected to the game world, fostering a sense of presence and agency.

- **Interactive Objects:**
  - **Clickable Objects:**
    - Implement object selection using raycasting from the mouse cursor.
    - Use collision detection to determine if the ray intersects with an object.
    - Example:
    - Python

```python
def check_click(task):
    if base.mouseWatcherNode.hasMouse()
and
base.mouseWatcherNode.isButtonDown(M
ouseButton.one()):
        mouse_pos =
base.mouseWatcherNode.getMouse()
        near_point = Point3()
        far_point = Point3()
        base.camLens.extrude(mouse_pos,
near_point, far_point)
        ray = CollisionRay(near_point,
far_point - near_point)
        queue = CollisionHandlerQueue()
        traverser = CollisionTraverser()

traverser.addCollider(CollisionNodePath(Co
llisionNode('ray')), queue)
        traverser.traverse(render)
        if queue.getNumEntries() > 0:
            queue.sortEntries()
            entry = queue.getEntry(0)
            clicked_object =
entry.getIntoNodePath().getParent()
```

```
    # Handle clicked object
    return task.cont
taskMgr.add(check_click, 'click_task')
```

- ■
- ■
- ○ **Trigger Volumes:**
  - ■ Use collision volumes to detect when the player enters or exits a specific area.
  - ■ Trigger events based on player proximity.
  - ■ Example:
  - ■ Python

```
trigger_node = CollisionNode('trigger')
```

```
trigger_node.addSolid(CollisionSphere(0,
0, 0, 5))
trigger_np                          =
render.attachNewNode(trigger_node)
trigger_np.setPos(10, 0, 0)
def check_trigger(task):
    queue = CollisionHandlerQueue()
    traverser = CollisionTraverser()

traverser.addCollider(player_collision_np,
queue)
    traverser.traverse(trigger_np)
    if queue.getNumEntries() > 0:
        # Player entered trigger
        pass
    return task.cont
taskMgr.add(check_trigger, 'trigger_task')
```

■

■

- ○ **Interactive Props:**

- Implement object manipulation, such as picking up, moving, or using objects.
- Use physics engines to simulate realistic interactions.[1]
- Example:
- Python

```python
def pickup_object(object_np):
    # Attach object to player's hand
    object_np.reparentTo(player_hand_np)
```

-
-

- **Dynamic Environments:**
  - **Environmental Effects:**

- Implement dynamic weather, day/night cycles, or environmental hazards.
- Use particle systems, shaders, and animations to create visual effects.
  - **Destructible Objects:**
    - Implement object destruction using physics simulations or animation sequences.
    - Use collision detection to trigger destruction events.
  - **Interactive Terrain:**
    - Implement terrain deformation, such as digging or building.
    - Use heightmaps and procedural generation techniques.
- **Contextual Interactions:**
  - **Context Menus:**
    - Display context-sensitive menus based on the

player's interaction with objects.

- ○ **Dialogue Systems:**
  - ■ Implement dialogue systems for interacting with NPCs.
  - ■ Use text-to-speech or pre-recorded audio for dialogue.
- ○ **Quick Time Events (QTEs):**
  - ■ Implement QTEs for cinematic or interactive sequences.

10.4 Building 3D User Interfaces (UI): Bridging the Gap

3D user interfaces provide players with information, feedback, and control within the 3D environment.[2] They enhance the player's understanding and interaction with the game world.

- **UI Elements:**
  - **Heads-Up Displays (HUDs):**
    - Display essential information, such as health, score, or inventory.
    - Use 2D overlays or 3D elements within the scene.
  - **Menus:**
    - Implement in-game menus for settings, inventory, or character customization.
    - Use 3D models or 2D textures for menu elements.
  - **Interactive Panels:**
    - Display information or controls on interactive panels within the 3D environment.
    - Use raycasting to interact with panels.
  - **3D Widgets:**

- Create 3D widgets for manipulating objects or displaying information.
- Use 3D models and animations for widgets.
- **UI Design Principles:**
  - **Clarity and Readability:**
    - Ensure that UI elements are easy to understand and read.
    - Use clear fonts and icons.
  - **Contextual Relevance:**
    - Display UI elements that are relevant to the current game state or context.
  - **Minimalism:**
    - Avoid clutter and unnecessary UI elements.
    - Focus on essential information.
  - **Visual Consistency:**
    - Maintain a consistent visual style throughout the UI.

- **Implementation Techniques:**
  - **2D Overlays:**
    - Use Panda3D's aspect2d or render2d nodes to create 2D overlays.
    - Draw textures and text onto the overlays.
  - **3D UI Elements:**
    - Create 3D models for UI elements.
    - Use raycasting to interact with 3D UI elements.
  - **GUI Libraries:**
    - Consider using GUI libraries or frameworks that integrate with Panda3D.
- **Interaction Methods:**
  - **Mouse Interaction:**
    - Use raycasting to interact with UI elements.
    - Implement hover effects and click events.
  - **Keyboard Interaction:**

- Use keyboard shortcuts or navigation keys to interact with UI elements.
  - **Gamepad Interaction:**
    - Use gamepad buttons and axes to interact with UI elements.

10.5 Implementing AI and Pathfinding in 3D Games: Smart Enemies and Dynamic Worlds

AI and pathfinding are essential for creating intelligent and challenging opponents and navigating complex 3D environments.[3]

- **AI Basics:**
  - **Behavior Trees:**
    - Use behavior trees to define complex AI behaviors.

- Behavior trees allow for hierarchical and modular AI logic.[4]
  - **Finite State Machines (FSMs):**
    - Use FSMs to manage AI states, such as idle, patrol, or attack.
  - **Sensors:**
    - Implement sensors for AI agents to perceive their environment.
    - Use raycasting or collision detection for sensors.
  - **Actions:**
    - Implement actions for AI agents to perform, such as moving, attacking, or interacting with objects.
- **Pathfinding:**
  - **Navigation Meshes (Navmeshes):**

- Use navmeshes to represent walkable areas in the 3D environment.
- Navmeshes simplify pathfinding calculations.
  - *A Algorithm:**
    - Use the A* algorithm to find the shortest path between two points on a navmesh.
    - Implement heuristics to guide the search.
  - **Path Following:**
    - Implement path following to make AI agents follow the calculated path.
  - **Obstacle Avoidance:**
    - Implement obstacle avoidance to prevent AI agents from colliding with objects.
    - Use raycasting or collision detection for obstacle avoidance.

- **AI Techniques:**
  - **Flocking Behavior:**
    - Implement flocking behavior for groups of AI agents.
    - Use rules for alignment, cohesion, and separation.
  - **Steering Behaviors:**
    - Implement steering behaviors for AI agents to navigate and interact with their environment.
    - Use behaviors such as seek, flee, and wander.
  - **Machine Learning:**
    - Use machine learning techniques to train AI agents to perform complex tasks.
    - Use reinforcement learning or neural networks.
- **Implementation Considerations:**
  - **Performance Optimization:**

- Optimize AI and pathfinding calculations for performance.
- Use efficient algorithms and data structures.
- **AI Debugging:**
  - Use debugging tools to visualize AI behavior and pathfinding.
  - Implement logging and visualization for AI state.
- **AI Balancing:**
  - Balance AI difficulty and behavior to create a challenging and engaging experience.

By mastering these techniques, you'll be well-prepared to create immersive and engaging 3D games with Panda3D.

Part V:

Comprehensive 3D Game Project and Deployment

CHAPTER 11

Designing and Developing a Complete 3D Game Project with Panda3D

Developing a complete 3D game project is a complex and rewarding endeavor. It requires a blend of creative vision, technical expertise, and meticulous planning. Panda3D provides a powerful platform for bringing your 3D game ideas to life, but a solid foundation is essential for success.

11.1 Project Planning and 3D Game Design: Laying the Groundwork

Effective project planning and thoughtful game design are crucial for a successful 3D game project. They provide a roadmap for development, ensuring that the final product aligns with the initial vision.

- **Conceptualization and Genre Definition:**
  - **Game Concept:** Clearly define the core idea of your game. What makes it unique and engaging?
  - **Genre Selection:** Choose a genre that aligns with your vision and technical capabilities. (e.g., RPG, FPS, puzzle, simulation).
  - **Target Audience:** Identify your target audience to tailor the game's design and features.
- **Game Design Document (GDD):**
  - **Gameplay Mechanics:** Define the core gameplay mechanics, including player actions, interactions, and challenges.
  - **Story and Narrative:** Develop a compelling story, characters, and world. (If applicable).
  - **Level Design:** Outline the structure and layout of levels,

including challenges, puzzles, and rewards.

- ○ **User Interface (UI) Design:** Plan the UI elements, layout, and interaction flow.
- ○ **Sound Design:** Specify the sound effects, music, and voice acting.
- ○ **Art Style and Visual Design:** Define the visual style, including character designs, environments, and effects.
- **Technical Design Document (TDD):**
  - ○ **Engine Features:** Identify the Panda3D features you will utilize.
  - ○ **Development Tools:** Select the tools for modeling, texturing, and animation.
  - ○ **Asset Pipeline:** Define the process for creating, managing, and integrating assets.

- o **Performance Optimization:** Plan for performance optimization techniques.
- o **Testing and Debugging:** Outline testing and debugging strategies.
- o **Build and Deployment:** Plan for the build and deployment process.
- **Project Scope and Timeline:**
  - o **Feature Prioritization:** Prioritize features based on their importance and feasibility.
  - o **Milestone Planning:** Break down the project into manageable milestones.
  - o **Resource Allocation:** Allocate resources (time, personnel, budget) effectively.
  - o **Risk Management:** Identify potential risks and develop mitigation strategies.
- **Prototyping and Iteration:**

- Early Prototyping: Create a basic prototype to test core gameplay mechanics.
- Iterative Development: Embrace an iterative development process, incorporating feedback and making adjustments.
- Playtesting: Conduct regular playtests to gather feedback and refine the game.

11.2 Creating 3D Game Assets and Environments: Building the World

Creating high-quality 3D game assets and environments is a crucial part of 3D game development. Panda3D provides tools and techniques to bring your visual vision to life.

- **3D Modeling:**

- **Modeling Software:** Choose a 3D modeling software (e.g., Blender, Maya, 3ds Max).
- **Modeling Techniques:** Use appropriate modeling techniques (e.g., polygonal modeling, sculpting).
- **Low-Poly vs. High-Poly:** Balance visual quality with performance by using low-poly models for distant objects and high-poly models for close-up details.
- **Optimization:** Optimize models for performance by reducing polygon count and using LODs (Level of Detail).

- **Texturing and Materials:**
  - **Texture Creation:** Create textures using image editing software (e.g., Photoshop, GIMP).
  - **Material Creation:** Define material properties (e.g., color,

shininess, reflectivity) using Panda3D's material system.

- ○ **Texture Mapping:** Use UV mapping to apply textures to 3D models.
- ○ **Normal Maps and Specular Maps:** Use normal maps for detailed surface effects and specular maps for realistic reflections.
- **Animation:**
  - ○ **Skeletal Animation:** Use skeletal animation for characters and creatures.
  - ○ **Keyframe Animation:** Use keyframe animation for props and environmental objects.
  - ○ **Animation Blending and Transitions:** Implement smooth animation blending and transitions.
  - ○ **Animation Optimization:** Optimize animations for performance by reducing

keyframe count and using animation compression.

- **Environment Creation:**
  - **Terrain Generation:** Use heightmaps or procedural generation techniques to create terrain.
  - **Environment Modeling:** Model buildings, props, and other environmental elements.
  - **Lighting and Shadows:** Implement realistic lighting and shadows.
  - **Environment Optimization:** Optimize environments for performance by using LODs, occlusion culling, and batching.
- **Asset Pipeline:**
  - **Version Control:** Use version control (e.g., Git) to manage assets.
  - **Asset Organization:** Organize assets into a logical folder structure.

- o **Asset Export and Import:** Define a consistent asset export and import process.
- o **Asset Optimization:** Optimize assets for performance before importing them into Panda3D.
- **Level Design Tools:**
  - o **External Editors:** Integrate with external level editors (e.g., Tiled) for efficient level design.
  - o **In-Engine Tools:** Develop custom in-engine tools for level editing.
- **Collaboration and Communication:**
  - o **Asset Sharing:** Use asset sharing platforms (e.g., Google Drive, Dropbox) for collaboration.
  - o **Communication Tools:** Use communication tools (e.g., Slack, Discord) for team communication.

- o **Documentation:** Document asset creation processes and guidelines.
- **Iterative Asset Development:**
  - o **Feedback Loops:** Establish feedback loops with artists and designers.
  - o **Asset Refinement:** Refine assets based on feedback and playtesting.

By following these guidelines, you can create high-quality 3D game assets and environments that bring your game world to life. Remember to balance visual quality with performance optimization and maintain a consistent art style throughout your project.

11.3 Implementing Core 3D Game Mechanics

Implementing core 3D game mechanics is where your game's vision transforms into playable reality. This stage involves translating design concepts into functional code, creating engaging interactions and challenges.

- **Player Movement and Controls:**
  - **Character Controller:** Implement a robust character controller that handles movement, jumping, and other player actions.
  - **Camera Control:** Design intuitive camera controls, including first-person, third-person, or fixed perspectives.

- **Input Handling:** Efficiently manage keyboard, mouse, and gamepad input.[1]
- **Example (Character Movement):**
- Python

```python
def update_player_movement(task):
    keys = base.win.getKeyboardMap()
    if keys.get('w'):

player_node.setPos(player_node.getPos() +
player_node.getNetTransform().getMat().ge
tRow3(1)          *          move_speed          *
globalClock.getDt())
    # Handle other movement keys
    return task.cont
taskMgr.add(update_player_movement,
'player_movement_task')
```

- ○
- ○
- **Collision Detection and Physics:**
  - ○ **Collision Solids:** Implement collision solids (spheres, boxes, polygons) for objects in the scene.
  - ○ **Physics Engine Integration:** Integrate a physics engine (Bullet, PhysX) for realistic interactions.
  - ○ **Collision Responses:** Define how objects react to collisions (e.g., bouncing, sliding, breaking).
  - ○ **Example (Bullet Physics):**
  - ○ Python

```python
from panda3d.bullet import BulletWorld,
BulletRigidBodyNode, BulletSphereShape

physics_world = BulletWorld()
```

```
physics_world.setGravity(Vec3(0, 0, -9.81))

player_shape = BulletSphereShape(1)
player_body                           =
BulletRigidBodyNode('player_body')
player_body.addShape(player_shape)
player_node                           =
render.attachNewNode(player_body)
physics_world.attachRigidBody(player_bod
y)
```

- o
- o

- **Gameplay Mechanics:**
  - o **Core Mechanics:** Implement the core mechanics that define your game (e.g., shooting, puzzle-solving, platforming).
  - o **Game Rules:** Define and implement the rules of your game.
  - o **Progression System:** Design a progression system that

rewards players and keeps them engaged.

- ○ **Example (Shooting):**
- ○ Python

```
def shoot():
                    ray        =
CollisionRay(camera_node.getPos(),
camera_node.getNetTransform().getMat().g
etRow3(1))
    # Implement raycasting and collision
detection
  # Spawn projectile
```

- ○
- ○

- **AI and Pathfinding:**
  - ○ **AI Behaviors:** Implement AI behaviors for enemies and NPCs (e.g., patrol, attack, flee).

- **Pathfinding:** Use navigation meshes and algorithms (A*) for AI pathfinding.
- **Example (AI Pathfinding):**
- Python

```
# Use a navigation mesh and A* algorithm
to find a path
# Move the AI agent along the path
```

-
-

- **Game Logic and State Management:**
  - **Game States:** Implement game states (menu, gameplay, pause) using a state machine.
  - **Event Handling:** Use event handling to manage game events and interactions.

- **Data Management:** Implement a system for managing game data (player stats, inventory).
- **Example (Game State):**
- Python

```python
class GameState:
    def __init__(self, game):
        self.game = game
    def enter(self): pass
    def update(self, task): pass
    def exit(self): pass

class MenuState(GameState):
    def update(self, task):
        # Menu logic
        return task.cont
```

○

○

11.4 Optimizing Performance for 3D Games: Smooth and Responsive Gameplay

Performance optimization is crucial for ensuring a smooth and responsive gameplay experience, especially in 3D games.[2]

- **Profiling and Bottleneck Identification:**
  - **Profiling Tools:** Use profiling tools to identify performance bottlenecks.[3]
  - **Frame Rate Monitoring:** Monitor frame rates to identify performance issues.
  - **CPU and GPU Usage:** Analyze CPU and GPU usage to identify resource-intensive areas.[4]
- **Geometry Optimization:**

- Level of Detail (LOD): Use LODs to reduce the polygon count of distant objects.[5]
- Occlusion Culling: Use occlusion culling to prevent rendering of hidden objects.
- Batching: Batch draw calls to reduce CPU overhead.
- Geometry Simplification: Simplify complex geometry to reduce polygon count.

- **Texture Optimization:**
  - Texture Compression: Use texture compression to reduce memory usage.
  - Texture Atlases: Use texture atlases to reduce draw calls.
  - Mipmapping: Use mipmapping to prevent texture aliasing.
  - Texture Resolution: Use appropriate texture resolutions to balance visual quality and performance.

- **Rendering Optimization:**
  - **Shader Optimization:** Optimize shaders for performance.
  - **Lighting Optimization:** Use efficient lighting techniques.
  - **Shadow Optimization:** Optimize shadow rendering.
  - **Render Settings:** Adjust render settings (e.g., anti-aliasing) to balance visual quality and performance.
- **Physics Optimization:**
  - **Collision Shape Optimization:** Use efficient collision shapes.
  - **Physics Simulation Settings:** Adjust physics simulation settings to balance realism and performance.
  - **Physics Culling:** Use physics culling to prevent unnecessary physics calculations.
- **Code Optimization:**

- ○ **Algorithm Optimization:** Use efficient algorithms and data structures.
- ○ **Code Profiling:** Profile code to identify performance bottlenecks.
- ○ **Memory Management:** Optimize memory usage to prevent leaks and improve performance.
- **Asset Optimization:**
  - ○ **Asset Compression:** Compress assets (models, textures, sounds) to reduce file size.
  - ○ **Asset Streaming:** Stream assets to reduce loading times.
  - ○ **Asset Caching:** Cache assets to improve performance.

11.5 Testing, Debugging, and Polishing Your 3D Game: Ensuring Quality and Polish

Testing, debugging, and polishing are essential for creating a high-quality 3D game. They ensure that the game is stable, bug-free, and visually appealing.

- **Testing:**
    - **Unit Testing:** Write unit tests to verify the correctness of individual components.
    - **Integration Testing:** Test the interactions between different game components.
    - **Gameplay Testing:** Test the gameplay mechanics and progression.
    - **Performance Testing:** Test the game's performance on different hardware.

- o **Usability Testing:** Test the game's UI and controls for usability.
- **Debugging:**
  - o **Debugging Tools:** Use debugging tools (e.g., IDE debuggers, Panda3D's debugging tools).[6]
  - o **Logging:** Implement logging to track errors and events.
  - o **Error Handling:** Implement robust error handling to prevent crashes.
  - o **Visual Debugging:** Use visual debugging techniques to visualize game data and behavior.
- **Polishing:**
  - o **Visual Polish:** Refine the game's visuals, including models, textures, and lighting.
  - o **Sound Polish:** Refine the game's sound effects and music.

- ○ **Gameplay Polish:** Fine-tune the gameplay mechanics and progression.
- ○ **UI Polish:** Refine the UI elements and interactions.
- ○ **Performance Polish:** Optimize the game's performance for smooth gameplay.
- **User Feedback:**
  - ○ **Playtesting Feedback:** Gather feedback from playtesters.
  - ○ **Bug Reporting:** Implement a system for bug reporting.
  - ○ **Community Feedback:** Engage with the community and gather feedback.
- **Iterative Refinement:**
  - ○ **Bug Fixing:** Fix bugs and issues reported by testers and players.
  - ○ **Feature Refinement:** Refine features based on feedback and testing.

- ○ **Content Refinement:** Refine game content (levels, assets) based on feedback and testing.
- **Release Preparation:**
  - ○ **Build and Packaging:** Create a build and package the game for distribution.
  - ○ **Documentation:** Create documentation for the game.
  - ○ **Release Testing:** Conduct final release testing.

By following these guidelines, you can create a high-quality 3D game project with Panda3D that is engaging, polished, and ready for release.

CHAPTER 12

Advanced Panda3D Techniques and Optimization

Advanced Panda3D techniques and optimization are crucial for creating visually stunning and performant 3D games. These techniques allow developers to push the boundaries of visual fidelity and create immersive experiences that captivate players.

12.1 Using Panda3D's Particle Systems: Adding Dynamic Visuals

Particle systems are essential for creating dynamic visual effects, such as explosions, smoke, fire, and weather.[1] Panda3D provides a flexible and powerful particle system that allows developers to create a wide range of effects.[2]

- **Particle System Basics:**
  - **Particle Emitters:** Particle systems consist of emitters that generate particles.[3]
  - **Particle Renderers:** Renderers control how particles are drawn.
  - **Particle Factories:** Factories define the properties of particles.
  - **Particle Modifiers:** Modifiers alter particle properties over time.
- **Creating Particle Systems:**
  - **Particle File (.ptf):** Use a .ptf file to define particle system properties.
  - **Loading Particle Systems:** Load particle systems using base.loader.loadParticleSystem().
  - **Starting Particle Systems:** Start particle systems using particle_system.start().

- Stopping Particle Systems: Stop particle systems using particle_system.stop().
- **Example (Loading and Starting):**
- Python

```
particle_system                    =
base.loader.loadParticleSystem("particles/e
xplosion.ptf")
particle_system.reparentTo(render)
particle_system.setPos(0, 10, 0)
particle_system.start()
```

-
-

- **Particle Emitters:**
  - **Point Emitters:** Emit particles from a single point.

- ○ **Box Emitters:** Emit particles from a box volume.
- ○ **Sphere Emitters:** Emit particles from a sphere volume.[4]
- ○ **Ring Emitters:** Emit particles from a ring.[5]
- ○ **Custom Emitters:** Create custom emitters using Python code.
- **Particle Renderers:**
  - ○ **Point Renderers:** Render particles as points.
  - ○ **Sprite Renderers:** Render particles as sprites (textures).
  - ○ **Line Renderers:** Render particles as lines.[6]
  - ○ **Geom Renderers:** Render particles as 3D geometry.
- **Particle Factories:**
  - ○ **Point Factories:** Create particles with basic properties.[7]
  - ○ **Sprite Factories:** Create particles with sprite textures.

- o **Oriented Sprite Factories:** Create particles that are oriented towards the camera.
- **Particle Modifiers:**
  - o **Color Modifiers:** Change particle colors over time.
  - o **Size Modifiers:** Change particle sizes over time.
  - o **Velocity Modifiers:** Change particle velocities over time.
  - o **Force Modifiers:** Apply forces to particles.
  - o **Lifespan Modifiers:** Change particle lifespans.
- **Particle System Optimization:**
  - o **Particle Count:** Reduce the number of particles to improve performance.
  - o **Particle Size:** Reduce particle sizes to improve performance.
  - o **Particle Textures:** Use optimized particle textures.

- ○ **Particle Blending:** Use appropriate particle blending modes.
- ○ **Particle Culling:** Cull particles that are outside the view frustum.
- **Advanced Particle Techniques:**
  - ○ **Particle Trails:** Create trails behind moving particles.
  - ○ **Particle Collisions:** Implement particle collisions with objects in the scene.
  - ○ **Particle Interactions:** Implement interactions between particles.
  - ○ **Particle Effects Libraries:** Use particle effects libraries for pre-made effects.

12.2 Implementing Advanced Shaders and Visual Effects: Enhancing Visual Realism

Shaders are essential for creating advanced visual effects and enhancing the realism of 3D scenes.[8] Panda3D supports GLSL shaders, allowing developers to create a wide range of effects.[9]

- **Shader Basics:**
    - **Vertex Shaders:** Process vertex data and transform vertices.
    - **Fragment Shaders:** Process fragment data and determine pixel colors.[10]
    - **GLSL (OpenGL Shading Language):** Panda3D uses GLSL for shaders.[11]
    - **Shader Attributes:** Pass data to shaders using attributes and uniforms.[12]
- **Creating Shaders:**

- **Shader Files (.glsl):** Create shader files using GLSL code.
- **Loading Shaders:** Load shaders using Shader.load().
- **Applying Shaders:** Apply shaders to nodes using node.setShader().
- **Example (Loading and Applying):**
- Python

```
shader = Shader.load(Shader.SL_GLSL,

vertex="shaders/my_vertex.glsl",

fragment="shaders/my_fragment.glsl")
model.setShader(shader)
```

-
-

- **Vertex Shaders:**
  - **Vertex Transformations:** Perform vertex transformations, such as rotation, scaling, and translation.
  - **Vertex Lighting:** Perform vertex lighting calculations.
  - **Vertex Attributes:** Pass vertex attributes to fragment shaders.
- **Fragment Shaders:**
  - **Pixel Color Calculation:** Calculate pixel colors based on lighting, textures, and other data.
  - **Texture Sampling:** Sample textures to determine pixel colors.
  - **Fragment Attributes:** Pass fragment attributes to the rendering pipeline.
- **Shader Uniforms:**
  - **Passing Data to Shaders:** Pass data to shaders using uniforms.

- Uniform Types: Use various
  uniform types, such as floats,
  vectors, and matrices.
- Setting Uniforms: Set
  uniform values using
  node.setShaderInput().

- **Advanced Shader Techniques:**
  - **Lighting and Shadows:**
    Implement advanced lighting
    and shadow techniques, such as
    deferred shading and shadow
    mapping.
  - **Post-Processing Effects:**
    Implement post-processing
    effects, such as bloom, blur, and
    color grading.[13]
  - **Material Shaders:** Create
    custom material shaders for
    specific surfaces.
  - **Geometry Shaders:** Use
    geometry shaders to generate
    new geometry.
  - **Compute Shaders:** Use
    compute shaders for

general-purpose GPU computing.

- **Visual Effects:**
  - **Water Effects:** Create realistic water effects using shaders.
  - **Fire Effects:** Create realistic fire effects using shaders and particle systems.
  - **Weather Effects:** Create realistic weather effects using shaders and particle systems.
  - **Distortion Effects:** Create distortion effects using shaders.
  - **Procedural Textures:** Create procedural textures using shaders.
- **Shader Optimization:**
  - **Shader Complexity:** Reduce shader complexity to improve performance.[14]
  - **Texture Sampling:** Minimize texture sampling operations.
  - **Shader Uniforms:** Minimize the number of shader uniforms.

- ○ **Shader Culling:** Cull shaders that are not visible.
- • **Shader Debugging:**
  - ○ **Shader Debugging Tools:** Use shader debugging tools to identify and fix shader errors.
  - ○ **Shader Logging:** Implement shader logging to track shader behavior.

By mastering these advanced techniques, you can create visually stunning and performant 3D games with Panda3D.

12.3 Profiling and Optimizing Panda3D Applications

Profiling and optimization are crucial for ensuring that your Panda3D applications run smoothly and efficiently. This involves identifying performance bottlenecks and implementing strategies to improve performance.

- **Profiling Techniques:**
  - **Frame Rate Monitoring:** Track the frame rate (FPS) to identify performance dips.
  - **CPU Profiling:** Use tools like cProfile (Python) or gprof (C++) to identify CPU-intensive sections of code.
  - **GPU Profiling:** Use graphics profiling tools (e.g., RenderDoc, NVIDIA Nsight) to identify GPU-bound operations.[1]
  - **Panda3D's Built-in Profiler:** Panda3D provides built-in profiling tools through the ShowBase class and the taskMgr.
  - **Example   (Panda3D Profiling):**
  - Python

```python
from direct.showbase.ShowBase import ShowBase
from panda3d.core import loadPrcFileData

loadPrcFileData("", "show-frame-rate-meter 1") # Enable frame rate meter
loadPrcFileData("", "task-timer-verbose 1") # Enable task timer output

class MyApp(ShowBase):
    def __init__(self):
        ShowBase.__init__(self)

        def my_task(task):
            # Some time-consuming operation
            return task.cont

        taskMgr.add(my_task, "my_task")

app = MyApp()
app.run()
```

○

- o

- **Optimization Strategies:**
  - o **Geometry Optimization:**
    - **Level of Detail (LOD):** Use LODs to reduce the polygon count of distant objects.
    - **Occlusion Culling:** Prevent rendering of hidden objects.[2]
    - **Geometry Simplification:** Reduce the complexity of geometry.[3]
    - **Batching:** Combine multiple draw calls into a single call.
  - o **Texture Optimization:**
    - **Texture Compression:** Use texture compression to reduce memory usage.[4]
    - **Texture Atlases:** Combine multiple textures into a single texture atlas.

- **Mipmapping:** Use mipmapping to prevent texture aliasing.
- **Texture Resolution:** Use appropriate texture resolutions.
  - **Rendering Optimization:**
    - **Shader Optimization:** Optimize shader code.
    - **Lighting Optimization:** Use efficient lighting techniques.
    - **Shadow Optimization:** Optimize shadow rendering.
    - **Render Settings:** Adjust render settings (e.g., anti-aliasing).
  - **Physics Optimization:**
    - **Collision Shape Optimization:** Use efficient collision shapes.

- **Physics Simulation Settings:** Adjust physics simulation settings.
- **Physics Culling:** Prevent unnecessary physics calculations.
- **Code Optimization:**
  - **Algorithm Optimization:** Use efficient algorithms and data structures.
  - **Code Profiling:** Identify and optimize performance-critical code sections.
  - **Memory Management:** Optimize memory usage.
- **Asset Optimization:**
  - **Asset Compression:** Compress assets (models, textures, sounds).
  - **Asset Streaming:** Load assets on demand.

- **Asset Caching:** Cache frequently used assets.
- **Optimization Tools:**
  - **RenderDoc:** A powerful graphics debugger and profiler.[5]
  - **NVIDIA Nsight:** A suite of tools for GPU profiling and debugging.[6]
  - **Intel VTune Profiler:** A CPU and GPU profiler.[7]
  - **Panda3D's Performance Monitor:** A built-in tool for monitoring performance metrics.[8]

12.4 Integrating External Libraries and Plugins: Extending Functionality

Panda3D's extensibility allows you to integrate external libraries and plugins to enhance its functionality.[9]

- **Python Libraries:**
  - **Using** pip**:** Install Python libraries using pip.
  - **Importing Libraries:** Import libraries into your Panda3D code.
  - **Example (Using NumPy):**
  - Python

```
import numpy as np
# Use NumPy for numerical computations
```

  -
  -
- **C++ Libraries:**
  - **Creating Bindings:** Use tools like SWIG or Cython to create Python bindings for C++ libraries.

- ○ **Building Plugins:** Build C++ plugins that can be loaded by Panda3D.
- ○ **Example (Using a C++ Physics Library):**
  - ■ Create bindings to the library.
  - ■ Build a plugin that exposes the library's functionality to Panda3D.
- **Panda3D Plugins:**
  - ○ **Loading Plugins:** Load plugins using loadPrcFileData() or loadPlugin().
  - ○ **Plugin Types:** Plugins can extend Panda3D's functionality in various ways, such as adding new node types, renderers, or physics engines.
  - ○ **Community Plugins:** Explore community-developed plugins for Panda3D.
- **External Engines:**

- **Integrating with Other Engines:** Integrate Panda3D with other engines, such as physics engines or game logic engines.[10]
- **Example (Integrating with a Game Logic Engine):**
  - Use a game logic engine to manage game states and logic.
  - Use Panda3D for rendering and input handling.

- **Asset Pipelines:**
  - **Integrating with Asset Creation Tools:** Integrate Panda3D with asset creation tools (e.g., Blender, Maya).
  - **Automation:** Automate asset import and export processes.

- **Interprocess Communication:**
  - **Sockets:** Use sockets for communication between Panda3D and other applications.

- Message Queues: Use message queues for asynchronous communication.

12.5 Creating Networked 3D Games (Basic Concepts): Connecting Players

Networked 3D games allow players to interact with each other in a shared 3D environment. Panda3D provides tools and techniques for creating networked games.[11]

- **Networking Basics:**
    - **Client-Server Architecture:** Use a client-server architecture for networked games.
    - **Network Protocols:** Use network protocols, such as TCP or UDP, for communication.
    - **Data Serialization:** Serialize game data for transmission over the network.

- ○ **Latency and Bandwidth:** Consider latency and bandwidth limitations.
- **Panda3D Networking:**
  - ○ **DirectNet:** Panda3D provides the DirectNet networking library.
  - ○ **Third-Party Libraries:** Use third-party networking libraries, such as Twisted or Pygame's network support.
  - ○ **Example (Basic Networking):**
  - ○ Python

Use sockets or DirectNet to send and receive data
Implement game logic for handling network messages

- o
- o
- **Networked Game Concepts:**
  - **Player Synchronization:** Synchronize player positions, actions, and states.
  - **Object Synchronization:** Synchronize the state of game objects.
  - **Latency Compensation:** Implement techniques to compensate for network latency.
  - **Security:** Implement security measures to prevent cheating and hacking.
  - **Server Hosting:** Host game servers on dedicated servers or cloud platforms.
- **Networked Game Design:**
  - **Game Mechanics:** Design game mechanics that are suitable for networked play.

- o **Network Protocol Design:** Design efficient network protocols.
- o **Latency Management:** Design game mechanics that minimize the impact of latency.
- o **Scalability:** Design the game to support a large number of players.
- **Networked Game Testing:**
  - o **Local Network Testing:** Test the game on a local network.
  - o **Internet Testing:** Test the game over the internet.
  - o **Load Testing:** Test the game's performance under heavy load.

By mastering these advanced techniques, you can create high-quality, optimized, and networked 3D games with Panda3D.

CHAPTER 13

Cross-Platform Deployment and Distribution

Cross-platform deployment and distribution are essential for making your games accessible to a broader audience. By packaging your games for different operating systems and creating executable files, you can ensure that players on Windows, macOS, and Linux can enjoy your creations.

13.1 Packaging Pygame, Arcade, and Panda3D Games: Preparing for Distribution

Packaging your games involves bundling all the necessary files, including code, assets, and dependencies, into a single distributable package.

- **Pygame and Arcade Packaging:**
  - **Dependency Management:**
    - Identify all the dependencies your game relies on (Pygame, Arcade, and any other libraries).
    - Use `pip freeze > requirements.txt` to generate a list of installed packages.
  - **Asset Organization:**
    - Organize your game assets (images, sounds, fonts) into a logical folder structure.
    - Ensure that asset paths are relative to the game's executable.
  - **Data Files:**
    - Include any data files your game needs (e.g., configuration files, level data).
  - **Packaging Tools:**

- **PyInstaller:** A popular tool for creating standalone executables from Python applications.[1]
- **cx_Freeze:** Another tool for creating standalone executables.[2]
- **Zip Files:** Create a zip archive containing all the game files.
  - **Example (PyInstaller):**
  - Bash

```
pip install pyinstaller
pyinstaller --onefile your_game.py
--add-data "assets;assets" --add-data
"requirements.txt;."
```

○

- your_game.py is the main script.
- --onefile creates a single executable.
- --add-data "assets;assets" includes the assets folder.
- --add-data "requirements.txt;." adds the requirements file.

- **Panda3D Packaging:**
  - **Panda3D Deployment Tool:**
    - Panda3D provides a built-in deployment tool called deploy-ng.
    - This tool automatically packages your game and its dependencies.[3]
  - **Creating a Distribution:**
    - Use the deploy-ng command with the appropriate options.
    - Specify the main script, assets, and target platform.

- **Example (Panda3D Deploy-ng):**
  - Bash

```
deploy-ng --main-script your_game.py --build-dir dist --platforms win_x64,osx_10_64,linux_x64
```

  -
    - your_game.py is the main script.
    - --build-dir dist specifies the output directory.
    - --platforms win_x64,osx_10_64,linux_x64 specifies the target platforms.
  - **Panda3D Runtime:**
    - Panda3D requires its runtime libraries to be

included in the distribution.

- deploy-ng handles this automatically.

- **Asset Bundling:**
  - Panda3D's asset bundling system can be used to package assets into .mf files.
  - This improves loading times and reduces the number of files.

- **General Packaging Considerations:**
  - **File Size:** Optimize assets and code to reduce the size of the distribution.
  - **Installation Instructions:** Provide clear installation instructions for players.
  - **License Files:** Include license files for your game and any third-party libraries.

○ **ReadMe File:** Include a README.txt file with information about the game.

13.2 Creating Executable Files for Windows, macOS, and Linux: Platform-Specific Distributions

Creating executable files for different platforms ensures that players can run your games without installing Python or other dependencies.

- **Windows Executables:**
  - **PyInstaller or cx_Freeze:** Use PyInstaller or cx_Freeze to create .exe files.
  - **Inno Setup:** Use Inno Setup to create professional-looking installers.
  - **NSIS (Nullsoft Scriptable Install System):** Another installer creation tool.

- **Example (Inno Setup):**
  - Create an Inno Setup script (.iss file) to define the installer settings.
  - Compile the script to create an installer executable.
- **macOS Executables:**
  - **PyInstaller or cx_Freeze:** Use PyInstaller or cx_Freeze to create .app bundles.
  - **DMG Canvas:** Use DMG Canvas to create disk image installers (.dmg).
  - **Example (PyInstaller .app):**
  - Bash

```
pyinstaller --onefile --windowed
--icon=icon.icns your_game.py --add-data
"assets:assets"
```

- o
  - ■ --windowed creates a windowed application.
  - ■ --icon=icon.icns sets the application icon.
  - o **Code Signing:**
    - ■ Code sign your application to prevent macOS security warnings.
    - ■ Use Apple's codesign tool.
- **Linux Executables:**
  - o **PyInstaller or cx_Freeze:** Use PyInstaller or cx_Freeze to create executable files.[4]
  - o **AppImage:** Create AppImage packages for easy distribution.
  - o **Snap Packages:** Create Snap packages for Ubuntu and other Linux distributions.
  - o **Debian Packages (.deb):** Create Debian packages for Debian-based distributions.[5]

- ○ **RPM Packages (.rpm):** Create RPM packages for Red Hat-based distributions.
- ○ **Example (AppImage):**
  - ▪ Use appimagetool to create an AppImage package.
- **Platform-Specific Considerations:**
  - ○ **File Paths:** Use platform-independent file paths.
  - ○ **System Dependencies:** Include any system dependencies that are not included in the distribution.
  - ○ **Icon Files:** Provide icon files for different platforms (.ico for Windows, .icns for macOS, .png for Linux).
  - ○ **Testing:** Thoroughly test your executables on different platforms and hardware.
- **Distribution Platforms:**

- ○ **Steam:** Distribute your games on Steam.
- ○ **Itch.io:** Distribute your games on Itch.io.
- ○ **GameJolt:** Distribute your games on GameJolt.
- ○ **Websites:** Host your games on your own website.
- **Version Control:**
  - ○ Use version control (Git) to manage your game's source code and assets.
  - ○ This allows for easy collaboration and version tracking.
- **Documentation:**
  - ○ Provide clear documentation for your game, including installation instructions, controls, and gameplay information.
  - ○ Create a website or forum for support.

By following these guidelines, you can create cross-platform distributions of your Pygame, Arcade, and Panda3D games, reaching a wider audience and ensuring that players can enjoy your creations on their preferred platforms.

13.3 Distributing Games on Game Platforms (Steam, Itch.io)

Distributing your games on game platforms like Steam and Itch.io is a crucial step in reaching a wider audience and building a community around your creations. These platforms provide tools and services to help you market, sell, and manage your games.

- Steam Distribution:
  - **Steamworks:** Steamworks is a suite of tools and services provided by Valve for game developers.[1]
  - **Steam Direct:** Steam Direct is the process for submitting your game to Steam.

- **Application Submission:** Prepare your game for submission, including metadata, screenshots, videos, and builds.
- **Store Page Creation:** Create an engaging store page with compelling descriptions, visuals, and trailers.
- **Build Uploads:** Upload your game builds using the Steamworks SDK.
- **Beta Testing:** Utilize Steam's beta testing features to gather feedback and fix bugs.[2]
- **Community Features:** Leverage Steam's community features, such as forums, workshops, and achievements.[3]
- **Marketing and Promotion:** Utilize Steam's marketing tools and participate in Steam events and sales.[4]
- **Steamworks SDK:** The Steamworks SDK allows for the

integration of Steam features such as achievements, leaderboards, and multiplayer.[5]

- o **Steam Cloud:** Steam Cloud allows for the storing of user save games and settings.[6]
- o **Steam Workshop:** Steam Workshop allows users to create and share content for your game.[7]
- o **Steam Analytics:** Steam provides analytics to help you understand your player base.[8]
- Itch.io Distribution:
  - o **Indie-Friendly Platform:** Itch.io is a popular platform for indie game developers.[9]
  - o **Easy Uploads:** Upload your games easily using the Itch.io dashboard.
  - o **Customization:** Customize your game's page with themes, descriptions, and visuals.

- ○ **Pricing Options:** Set your own pricing options, including pay-what-you-want and free.
- ○ **Community Interaction:** Engage with the Itch.io community through forums and comments.
- ○ **Jam Support:** Itch.io is a great place to host and participate in game jams.
- ○ **Analytics:** Itch.io provides analytics to help you understand your player base.[10]
- ○ **Embeddable Games:** Itch.io supports embeddable HTML5 games.
- ○ **Bundles and Sales:** Itch.io supports game bundles and sales events.
- General Distribution Considerations:
  - ○ **Target Audience:** Tailor your game's marketing and promotion to your target audience.

- **Marketing Materials:** Create high-quality marketing materials, such as screenshots, trailers, and press releases.
- **Community Engagement:** Engage with your community through social media, forums, and Discord.
- **Localization:** Consider localizing your game for different languages.
- **Customer Support:** Provide excellent customer support to your players.
- **Legal Considerations:** Ensure that you have the necessary licenses and permissions for your game's assets and content.
- **Game Updates:** Plan for game updates and patches.
- **Pricing Strategy:** Develop a pricing strategy that is competitive and profitable.

13.4 Mobile Game Development Considerations (If Applicable): Expanding to Mobile

If you're considering porting your games to mobile platforms, there are several important considerations to keep in mind.

- Platform Choice:
  - **iOS:** Develop for iOS using Xcode and Swift or Objective-C.
  - **Android:** Develop for Android using Android Studio and Java or Kotlin.
  - **Cross-Platform Frameworks:** Use cross-platform frameworks like Unity, Unreal Engine, Godot, Kivy, or Beeware to develop for both iOS and Android.[11]
- Input Methods:
  - **Touch Controls:** Design intuitive touch controls for your game.

- ○ **Accelerometer and Gyroscope:** Utilize the accelerometer and gyroscope for motion controls.
  - ○ **Virtual Joysticks and Buttons:** Implement virtual joysticks and buttons for precise control.
- Screen Size and Resolution:
  - ○ **Responsive Design:** Design your UI and gameplay to adapt to different screen sizes and resolutions.[12]
  - ○ **Aspect Ratios:** Consider different aspect ratios and resolutions.
  - ○ **UI Scaling:** Implement UI scaling to ensure that UI elements are readable and usable on different devices.
- Performance Optimization:
  - ○ **Mobile Hardware Limitations:** Optimize your

game for mobile hardware limitations.[13]

- ○ **Memory Management:** Optimize memory usage to prevent crashes.
- ○ **Battery Life:** Optimize your game to minimize battery consumption.
- ○ **Texture Compression:** Use texture compression to reduce memory usage.[14]
- ○ **LODs (Level of Detail):** Use LODs to reduce the polygon count of distant objects.
- • Mobile-Specific Features:
  - ○ **In-App Purchases:** Implement in-app purchases for monetization.
  - ○ **Push Notifications:** Use push notifications to engage players.
  - ○ **Social Media Integration:** Integrate with social media platforms.

- o **Cloud Saves:** Implement cloud saves for cross-device synchronization.
- Mobile Development Tools:
  - o **Xcode (iOS):** Apple's integrated development environment for iOS development.[15]
  - o **Android Studio (Android):** Google's integrated development environment for Android development.[16]
  - o **Unity:** A popular cross-platform game engine.
  - o **Unreal Engine:** A powerful cross-platform game engine.[17]
  - o **Godot:** A free and open-source cross-platform game engine.[18]
  - o **Kivy:** A Python framework for creating cross-platform mobile apps.
  - o **Beeware:** A suite of tools to help develop native applications in Python.[19]

- Mobile Testing:
  - **Device Testing:** Test your game on a variety of mobile devices.
  - **Emulator Testing:** Use emulators for initial testing.
  - **Beta Testing:** Conduct beta testing to gather feedback from real users.
- Mobile Distribution:
  - **App Store (iOS):** Distribute your iOS games on the App Store.
  - **Google Play Store (Android):** Distribute your Android games on the Google Play Store.
  - **Third-Party App Stores:** Consider distributing your games on third-party app stores.
- Monetization Strategies:
  - **Free-to-Play:** Offer your game for free with in-app purchases or ads.

- Premium: Sell your game for a one-time purchase.
- Subscription: Offer a subscription service for access to exclusive content.
- Ad-Supported: Display ads within your game.

By carefully considering these factors, you can effectively distribute your games on game platforms and expand your reach to mobile audiences.

CHAPTER 14

Game Design Principles and Best Practices

Game design is the art and science of creating interactive experiences that entertain, challenge, and engage players.[1] It involves understanding core principles, crafting compelling narratives, and designing intuitive gameplay mechanics. By adhering to best practices, game developers can create games that are both enjoyable and memorable.[2]

14.1 Understanding Core Game Design Principles: Foundations of Engagement

Core game design principles provide a framework for creating games that are fun, engaging, and rewarding.[3] These principles guide the development process, ensuring that the final product aligns with the initial vision.[4]

- **Core Mechanics and Gameplay Loop:**
  - **Core Mechanics:** Define the fundamental actions and interactions that drive the gameplay.
  - **Gameplay Loop:** Create a repetitive cycle of actions and rewards that keeps players engaged.[5]
  - **Example:** In a platformer, the core mechanics might be jumping and running, while the gameplay loop involves navigating obstacles, collecting items, and reaching the goal.
- **Player Agency and Choice:**
  - **Meaningful Choices:** Provide players with choices that have significant consequences.[6]

- ○ **Player Agency:** Empower players to influence the game world and their own experience.[7]
- ○ **Example:** In an RPG, players might choose their character's class, skills, and dialogue options, shaping their journey through the game.[8]
- **Challenge and Difficulty:**
  - ○ **Balanced Difficulty:** Design challenges that are appropriately difficult for the target audience.[9]
  - ○ **Progression Curve:** Gradually increase the difficulty as players progress through the game.[10]
  - ○ **Skill-Based Challenges:** Emphasize skill-based challenges over luck-based ones.
  - ○ **Example:** A puzzle game might start with simple puzzles and gradually introduce more complex mechanics and obstacles.[11]
- **Feedback and Reward:**

- ○ **Clear Feedback:** Provide players with clear and immediate feedback for their actions.
- ○ **Meaningful Rewards:** Reward players for their accomplishments with meaningful rewards.
- ○ **Positive Reinforcement:** Use positive reinforcement to motivate players and encourage continued engagement.[12]
- ○ **Example:** A shooter might provide visual and auditory feedback for successful shots and reward players with points or unlockable items.[13]
- • **Narrative and Storytelling:**
  - ○ **Compelling Narrative:** Craft a compelling narrative that engages players emotionally.
  - ○ **Character Development:** Develop memorable characters

with distinct personalities and motivations.

- ○ **World-Building:** Create a rich and immersive game world with lore and history.
- ○ **Example:** An adventure game might tell a story of a hero's journey through a fantastical world, with memorable characters and plot twists.
- **User Interface (UI) and User Experience (UX):**
  - ○ **Intuitive UI:** Design a user interface that is easy to understand and use.
  - ○ **Clear Information:** Provide players with clear and concise information about the game state.
  - ○ **Positive UX:** Create a positive user experience that is enjoyable and frustration-free.
  - ○ **Example:** A strategy game might have a clean and

organized UI that allows players to easily manage their units and resources.[14]

- **Accessibility:**
  - **Inclusive Design:** Design games that are accessible to players with disabilities.[15]
  - **Customizable Controls:** Provide customizable controls and settings.[16]
  - **Visual and Auditory Aids:** Implement visual and auditory aids to improve accessibility.[17]
  - **Example:** A racing game might provide adjustable difficulty settings and customizable controls for players with different needs.
- **Playtesting and Iteration:**
  - **Regular Playtesting:** Conduct regular playtests with target audience members.

- ○ **Feedback Analysis:** Analyze playtest feedback and identify areas for improvement.
- ○ **Iterative Design:** Iterate on the game design based on feedback and data.[18]
- ○ **Example:** A platformer might undergo multiple rounds of playtesting to refine level design and gameplay mechanics.[19]
- **Innovation and Creativity:**
  - ○ **Unique Concepts:** Develop unique game concepts and mechanics.
  - ○ **Creative Problem-Solving:** Encourage creative problem-solving and experimentation.
  - ○ **Artistic Vision:** Express a strong artistic vision through the game's visuals and sound.
  - ○ **Example:** An indie game might experiment with unconventional gameplay mechanics or visual

styles to create a unique experience.

14.2 Level Design and Player Experience: Crafting Engaging Worlds

Level design is the art of creating immersive and engaging game environments that guide players through the gameplay experience.[20] It involves understanding player psychology, crafting compelling challenges, and creating a sense of progression.

- **Level Layout and Flow:**
    - **Clear Paths:** Design clear and intuitive paths for players to follow.
    - **Visual Cues:** Use visual cues to guide players and highlight important areas.

- o **Pacing and Rhythm:** Create a balanced pacing and rhythm to keep players engaged.[21]
- o **Example:** A level might start with a tutorial area, gradually introduce new mechanics, and culminate in a challenging boss fight.
- **Challenge and Obstacle Design:**
  - o **Varied Challenges:** Introduce a variety of challenges and obstacles to keep players engaged.
  - o **Meaningful Obstacles:** Design obstacles that are relevant to the game's mechanics and narrative.
  - o **Difficulty Progression:** Gradually increase the difficulty of challenges as players progress.[22]
  - o **Example:** A puzzle level might introduce new puzzle mechanics

and gradually increase the complexity of the puzzles.[23]

- **Exploration and Discovery:**
  - **Hidden Areas:** Include hidden areas and secrets for players to discover.
  - **Environmental Storytelling:** Use environmental details to tell a story and create atmosphere.
  - **Rewards for Exploration:** Reward players for exploring with items, secrets, or lore.
  - **Example:** A level might contain hidden collectibles, lore fragments, or alternate paths that reward exploration.
- **Player Guidance and Feedback:**
  - **Visual Cues:** Use visual cues to guide players and highlight important areas.
  - **Tutorials and Hints:** Provide tutorials and hints to help players understand the game mechanics.[24]

- o **Feedback for Actions:** Provide clear feedback for player actions and decisions.
- o **Example:** A level might use lighting or environmental details to guide players towards the objective.[25]
- **Atmosphere and Immersion:**
  - o **Visual Design:** Create a consistent visual style that enhances the atmosphere.
  - o **Sound Design:** Use sound effects and music to create a sense of immersion.[26]
  - o **Environmental Details:** Add environmental details to create a believable and engaging world.[27]
  - o **Example:** A horror level might use dim lighting, eerie sound effects, and disturbing environmental details to create a sense of dread.
- **Player Psychology and Motivation:**

- o **Sense of Accomplishment:** Design levels that provide players with a sense of accomplishment.
- o **Curiosity and Exploration:** Encourage curiosity and exploration by providing hidden areas and secrets.
- o **Challenge and Mastery:** Design levels that provide players with a sense of challenge and mastery.[28]
- o **Example:** A level might contain challenging puzzles that reward players with a sense of satisfaction upon completion.
- **Level Testing and Iteration:**
  - o **Playtesting:** Conduct regular playtests with target audience members.
  - o **Feedback Analysis:** Analyze playtest feedback and identify areas for improvement.

- Iterative Design: Iterate on the level design based on feedback and data.
- Example: A level might undergo multiple rounds of playtesting to refine the pacing, difficulty, and layout.

By adhering to these principles and best practices, game developers can create games that are not only fun and engaging but also meaningful and memorable.

14.3 Storytelling and Narrative in Games

Storytelling and narrative are powerful tools for creating immersive and emotionally resonant games. They can transform a simple gameplay experience into a memorable journey, engaging players on a deeper level.

- **Narrative Structures:**
  - **Linear Narrative:** A straightforward, chronological story progression.
  - **Branching Narrative:** Player choices lead to different story paths and endings.
  - **Emergent Narrative:** Stories arise from player interactions and system dynamics.[1]
  - **Environmental Storytelling:** Narrative conveyed through environmental details and clues.[2]
  - **Example:** A linear narrative might follow a hero's journey, while a branching narrative allows players to make choices that impact the outcome.[3]
- **Character Development:**
  - **Archetypes and Stereotypes:** Use archetypes as a starting point, but avoid relying on stereotypes.

- Backstory and Motivation: Develop rich backstories and motivations for characters.
  - **Backstory and Motivation:** Develop rich backstories and motivations for characters.
  - **Character Arcs:** Create character arcs that show growth and change over time.[4]
  - **Example:** A character might start as a reluctant hero and gradually embrace their destiny.
- **World-Building:**
  - **Lore and History:** Create a rich and detailed world with its own history, culture, and mythology.
  - **Consistency and Coherence:** Ensure that the world is consistent and coherent.
  - **Environmental Details:** Use environmental details to convey the world's history and atmosphere.
  - **Example:** A fantasy world might have its own pantheon of

gods, political factions, and magical systems.

- **Narrative Devices:**
  - **Dialogue and Exposition:** Use dialogue and exposition to convey information and advance the story.
  - **Cutscenes and Cinematics:** Use cutscenes and cinematics to create dramatic moments.
  - **In-Game Events:** Use in-game events to trigger narrative moments.
  - **Example:** A cutscene might reveal a character's backstory, while an in-game event might trigger a boss fight.
- **Player Agency and Choice:**
  - **Meaningful Choices:** Provide players with choices that have significant consequences.[5]
  - **Impact on Narrative:** Allow player choices to impact the narrative and world.

- ○ **Moral Dilemmas:** Present players with moral dilemmas that force them to make difficult choices.
- ○ **Example:** A player might choose to side with one faction over another, impacting the game's ending.
- **Emotional Engagement:**
  - ○ **Empathy and Connection:** Create characters and situations that players can empathize with.[6]
  - ○ **Emotional Arcs:** Craft emotional arcs for characters and the player.[7]
  - ○ **Suspense and Tension:** Build suspense and tension to keep players engaged.
  - ○ **Example:** A game might explore themes of loss, grief, or redemption.[8]
- **Narrative Integration with Gameplay:**

- o **Ludonarrative Harmony:** Ensure that the narrative and gameplay mechanics are aligned.
- o **Narrative Mechanics:** Use gameplay mechanics to tell the story.
- o **Example:** A puzzle game might use puzzles to reveal clues about the narrative.
- **Narrative Design Tools:**
  - o **Scriptwriting Software:** Use scriptwriting software to write dialogue and cutscenes.
  - o **Interactive Storytelling Tools:** Use interactive storytelling tools to create branching narratives.
  - o **World-Building Tools:** Use world-building tools to organize lore and history.
- **Narrative Testing and Iteration:**
  - o **Playtesting:** Conduct playtests to gather feedback on the narrative.

- Feedback Analysis: Analyze feedback and identify areas for improvement.
- Iterative Refinement: Refine the narrative based on feedback and data.

14.4 Monetization Strategies (If Applicable): Generating Revenue

Monetization strategies are crucial for game developers who want to generate revenue from their games.[9] The right strategy can help you sustain your development efforts and reach a wider audience.

- **Premium Model:**
  - **One-Time Purchase:** Players pay a one-time fee to purchase the game.
  - **No In-App Purchases:** No additional purchases are required to access the full game.

- o **Target Audience:** Suitable for games with a strong narrative or unique gameplay.
- o **Example:** Indie games on Steam or console games.
- **Free-to-Play Model:**
  - o **Free Download:** Players can download and play the game for free.
  - o **In-App Purchases (IAPs):** Players can purchase virtual items, currency, or content.[10]
  - o **Advertising:** Display ads within the game.
  - o **Target Audience:** Suitable for mobile games or games with a large player base.
  - o **Example:** Mobile games with cosmetic items or level skips.
- **Subscription Model:**
  - o **Recurring Payments:** Players pay a recurring fee for access to the game or content.[11]

- Exclusive **Content:**
  Subscribers receive exclusive content or benefits.
- **Target Audience:** Suitable for MMOs or games with ongoing content updates.
- **Example:** MMOs with monthly subscriptions.

- **Ad-Supported Model:**
  - **Free Play:** Players can play the game for free with ads.
  - **Ad Revenue:** Developers earn revenue from ad impressions and clicks.[12]
  - **Target Audience:** Suitable for casual games or mobile games.
  - **Example:** Mobile games with banner ads or interstitial ads.

- **Cosmetic Items:**
  - **Visual Customization:** Players can purchase cosmetic items to customize their characters or items.[13]

- o **No Gameplay Impact:** Cosmetic items do not affect gameplay balance.
- o **Target Audience:** Suitable for multiplayer games or games with character customization.
- o **Example:** Skins, emotes, or character outfits.
- **Battle Passes:**
  - o **Tiered Rewards:** Players can purchase a battle pass to unlock tiered rewards by completing challenges.[14]
  - o **Time-Limited Content:** Battle passes offer time-limited content.
  - o **Target Audience:** Suitable for games with ongoing content updates.
  - o **Example:** Multiplayer games with seasonal battle passes.
- **Ethical Considerations:**

- Avoid **Pay-to-Win:** Ensure that monetization strategies do not create a pay-to-win system.
- **Transparency:** Be transparent about monetization practices.
- **Player Experience:** Prioritize the player experience over revenue generation.[15]

14.5 Building a Game Development Portfolio: Showcasing Your Skills

A strong game development portfolio is essential for showcasing your skills and experience to potential employers or clients.[16] It provides evidence of your abilities and creativity.

- **Portfolio Components:**
    - **Personal Website:** Create a professional website to showcase your work.

- Game Projects: Include a variety of game projects that demonstrate your skills.[17]
- **Source Code:** Provide links to source code repositories (GitHub).
- **Art Assets:** Include art assets that you have created (models, textures, animations).[18]
- **Game Design Documents:** Include game design documents that demonstrate your design process.[19]
- **Resume and Cover Letter:** Include a resume and cover letter that highlight your skills and experience.
- **Project Selection:**
  - **Variety:** Include a variety of projects that showcase your skills in different areas (programming, art, design).
  - **Quality over Quantity:** Focus on quality over quantity.

- **Personal Projects:** Include personal projects that demonstrate your passion and creativity.
- **Presentation:**
  - **Visual Appeal:** Design a visually appealing portfolio website.
  - **Clear Descriptions:** Provide clear descriptions of your projects.
  - **Gameplay Videos:** Include gameplay videos to showcase your games.
  - **User-Friendly Navigation:** Ensure that your portfolio is easy to navigate.
- **Networking:**
  - **Online Communities:** Participate in online game development communities.
  - **Game Jams:** Participate in game jams to build your portfolio and network.[20]

- ○ **Industry Events:** Attend industry events to network with other developers.[21]
- **Continuous Improvement:**
  - ○ **Update Regularly:** Update your portfolio with new projects and skills.
  - ○ **Seek Feedback:** Seek feedback from other developers and professionals.
  - ○ **Learn New Skills:** Continuously learn new skills and technologies.

By following these guidelines, you can build a strong game development portfolio that showcases your skills and helps you land your dream job or project.

CHAPTER 15

Future Trends in Python Game Development

The landscape of game development is constantly evolving, driven by technological advancements and changing player expectations. Python, with its versatility and growing ecosystem, is well-positioned to adapt to these trends.[1] Understanding emerging technologies and advancements in game engines and libraries is crucial for Python game developers to stay relevant and create innovative experiences.

15.1 Emerging Technologies (VR/AR, Cloud Gaming): Expanding the Boundaries of Immersion

Virtual Reality (VR), Augmented Reality (AR), and cloud gaming are revolutionizing the way we experience games.[2] These technologies offer new possibilities for immersion, interactivity, and accessibility.[3]

- Virtual Reality (VR):
    - Immersive Experiences: VR creates immersive, three-dimensional environments that transport players into the game world.[4]
    - Motion Tracking: VR headsets and controllers track player movements, allowing for natural interactions.[5]
    - Applications: VR is used for various game genres, including simulations, exploration, and first-person experiences.
    - Python Integration: Python can be used to develop VR experiences using libraries like PyOpenVR and OpenVR Python bindings.[6]
    - Challenges: VR development requires careful consideration of

performance, motion sickness, and user interface design.[7]

- Augmented Reality (AR):
    - Overlaying Digital Content: AR overlays digital content onto the real world, creating interactive experiences.[8]
    - Mobile AR: Mobile AR apps use smartphone cameras and sensors to create AR experiences.[9]
    - AR Headsets: AR headsets like HoloLens and Magic Leap provide hands-free AR experiences.[10]
    - Applications: AR is used for games, educational apps, and industrial applications.[11]
    - Python Integration: Python can be used to develop AR experiences using libraries like ARKit Python bindings (for iOS) and ARCore Python bindings (for Android).

- Challenges: AR development requires accurate tracking, occlusion handling, and seamless integration with the real world.[12]
- Cloud Gaming:
  - Streaming Games: Cloud gaming platforms stream games to players over the internet, eliminating the need for high-end hardware.[13]
  - Accessibility: Cloud gaming makes games accessible to players on various devices, including smartphones, tablets, and smart TVs.[14]
  - Scalability: Cloud gaming platforms can scale to support a large number of players.[15]
  - Applications: Cloud gaming is used for streaming AAA games, indie games, and casual games.[16]
  - Python Integration: Python can be used to develop cloud gaming

services and tools, such as server-side logic and game management systems.

- ○ Challenges: Cloud gaming requires low latency, high bandwidth, and reliable infrastructure.[17]
- Python's Role:
  - ○ Prototyping: Python's rapid prototyping capabilities make it ideal for developing VR/AR and cloud gaming prototypes.[18]
  - ○ Data Analysis: Python's data analysis libraries can be used to analyze player data and optimize game performance.
  - ○ Server-Side Logic: Python can be used to develop server-side logic for multiplayer VR/AR and cloud gaming experiences.
  - ○ AI and Machine Learning: Python's AI and machine learning libraries can be used to

create intelligent VR/AR and cloud gaming experiences.[19]

- Cross-Platform Development: Python's cross-platform capabilities make it suitable for developing VR/AR and cloud gaming applications for multiple platforms.[20]

15.2 Advances in Game Engines and Libraries: Empowering Python Game Development

Game engines and libraries are constantly evolving, providing developers with new tools and features to create more sophisticated and engaging games.

- Game Engine Advancements:
  - Real-Time Ray Tracing: Real-time ray tracing provides more realistic lighting and shadows.[21]
  - Procedural Generation: Procedural generation

techniques create dynamic and varied game content.[22]

- ○ AI and Machine Learning Integration: Game engines are increasingly integrating AI and machine learning capabilities.[23]
- ○ Cloud Integration: Game engines are integrating with cloud platforms to provide cloud-based features.[24]
- ○ Python Integration: More game engines are providing Python scripting support or integration.
- Python Game Libraries:
  - ○ Pygame Enhancements: Pygame is continuously being updated with new features and improvements.
  - ○ Arcade Expansion: Arcade is expanding its capabilities with new features for 3D game development and advanced UI.
  - ○ Panda3D Evolution: Panda3D is evolving with new features for

rendering, physics, and networking.[25]

- New Libraries: New Python game libraries are emerging, providing developers with more options.
- Example: Libraries that provide enhanced GUI options, or that simplify complex mathematical operations for game development.

- Cross-Platform Development:
  - Improved Cross-Platform Tools: Cross-platform development tools are becoming more robust and easier to use.
  - WebAssembly (WASM): WASM allows for running Python games in web browsers.
  - Mobile Development: Python frameworks like Kivy and Beeware are making it easier to develop mobile games.[26]
- AI and Machine Learning:

- Reinforcement Learning: Reinforcement learning is being used to train AI agents in games.[27]
- Procedural Content Generation: Machine learning is being used to generate game content procedurally.[28]
- Player Behavior Analysis: Machine learning is being used to analyze player behavior and personalize game experiences.[29]

- Cloud Gaming Technologies:
  - Low-Latency Streaming: Technologies for low-latency game streaming are improving.
  - Edge Computing: Edge computing is being used to reduce latency in cloud gaming.[30]
  - Scalable Server Architectures: Scalable server architectures are being developed to support a large number of players.[31]

- Community and Ecosystem:
  - Growing Community: The Python game development community is growing, providing more resources and support.[32]
  - Open-Source Contributions: More developers are contributing to open-source Python game libraries and tools.
  - Educational Resources: More educational resources are becoming available for Python game development.
- Future Trends:
  - Metaverse Integration: Python may play a role in developing metaverse experiences.[33]
  - Blockchain and NFTs: Python may be used to develop blockchain-based games and NFTs.[34]
  - AI-Generated Content: AI may be used to generate game

content, such as levels, characters, and stories.[35]

- ○ Accessibility and Inclusivity: Game development will focus more on accessibility and inclusivity.

By staying informed about these trends and manadvancements, Python game developers can create innovative and engaging games that push the boundaries of interactive entertainment.

15.3 The Role of Python in Future Game Development

Python's versatility, ease of use, and growing ecosystem make it well-suited for a variety of roles in the future of game development.[1] While not always the primary language for high-performance game engines, its applications are vast and growing.

- **Rapid Prototyping and Iteration:**
  - ○ **Speed of Development:** Python's concise syntax and

extensive libraries allow for rapid prototyping and iteration, enabling developers to quickly test game concepts and mechanics.[2]

- **Agile Development:** Python's flexibility supports agile development methodologies, allowing for frequent changes and updates.[3]
- **Example:** Python can be used to create quick prototypes of gameplay mechanics, UI layouts, or AI behaviors.

- **Tool Development and Automation:**
  - **Content Pipelines:** Python can be used to automate content pipelines, such as asset processing, level generation, and build automation.
  - **Custom Tools:** Developers can create custom tools for level

design, animation, and other game development tasks.[4]

- **Example:** Python scripts can automate the process of converting 3D models to a specific format or generating texture atlases.[5]

- **Data Analysis and Game Analytics:**
  - **Player Behavior Analysis:** Python's data analysis libraries (NumPy, Pandas, Scikit-learn) can be used to analyze player behavior and identify patterns.
  - **Game Performance Monitoring:** Python can be used to monitor game performance and identify bottlenecks.[6]
  - **A/B Testing:** Python can be used to conduct A/B testing and optimize game features.[7]
  - **Example:** Python scripts can analyze player data to identify

popular game modes or optimize in-game economy.

- **Artificial Intelligence and Machine Learning:**
  - **AI Agents:** Python's AI and machine learning libraries (TensorFlow, PyTorch) can be used to develop intelligent AI agents.[8]
  - **Procedural Content Generation:** Machine learning can be used to generate game content procedurally.[9]
  - **Reinforcement Learning:** Reinforcement learning can be used to train AI agents to perform complex tasks.[10]
  - **Example:** Python can be used to train AI agents to navigate complex environments or play games against human players.
- **Server-Side Development and Cloud Gaming:**

- ○ **Backend Services:** Python can be used to develop backend services for multiplayer games and cloud gaming platforms.[11]
- ○ **Game Servers:** Python's networking libraries can be used to develop game servers.[12]
- ○ **Cloud Integration:** Python can be used to integrate games with cloud platforms.[13]
- ○ **Example:** Python can be used to develop server-side logic for player authentication, matchmaking, and data storage.[14]
- **Virtual Reality (VR) and Augmented Reality (AR):**
  - ○ **Prototyping:** Python can be used to develop VR/AR prototypes and experiments.[15]
  - ○ **Data Processing:** Python can be used to process sensor data and create interactive experiences.[16]

- Example: Python can be used to develop VR simulations or AR applications for mobile devices.[17]
- **Educational and Indie Game Development:**
  - **Accessibility:** Python's ease of use and readability make it ideal for educational and indie game development.[18]
  - **Rapid Development:** Python allows for rapid development, making it suitable for game jams and short-term projects.[19]
  - **Example:** Python can be used to create educational games or indie games with unique gameplay mechanics.[20]
- **Cross-Platform Development:**
  - **Frameworks and Libraries:** Python frameworks like Kivy and Beeware allow for cross-platform development.[21]
  - **WebAssembly (WASM):** Python can be compiled to

WASM, allowing for running games in web browsers.[22]

- **Example:** Python can be used to develop games that can be deployed on multiple platforms, including desktop, mobile, and web.

- **Emerging Technologies:**
  - **Metaverse Integration:** Python may play a role in developing metaverse experiences.[23]
  - **Blockchain and NFTs:** Python can be used to develop blockchain-based games and NFTs.[24]
  - **AI-Generated Content:** AI may be used to generate game content, such as levels, characters, and stories.[25]
  - **Example:** Python can be used to develop tools for creating and managing NFTs or generating

procedural content for metaverse environments.[26]

- **Community and Ecosystem:**
  - **Growing Community:** The Python game development community is growing, providing more resources and support.[27]
  - **Open-Source Contributions:** More developers are contributing to open-source Python game libraries and tools.
  - **Educational Resources:** More educational resources are becoming available for Python game development.

15.4 Community and Resources for Continued Learning: Fostering Growth and Collaboration

The game development community and available resources are essential for continued learning and growth. They provide opportunities for collaboration, knowledge sharing, and skill development.

- **Online Communities:**
    - **Forums and Discussion Boards:** Participate in online forums and discussion boards to ask questions and share knowledge.[28]
    - **Social Media Groups:** Join social media groups to connect with other game developers.
    - **Discord Servers:** Join Discord servers to chat with other developers in real-time.

- ○ **Reddit Communities:** Explore Reddit communities dedicated to game development and Python.
- ○ **Example:** r/gamedev, r/python, r/pygame, r/panda3d, r/arcade.
- **Online Resources:**
  - ○ **Documentation:** Refer to official documentation for game engines and libraries.
  - ○ **Tutorials and Courses:** Take online tutorials and courses to learn new skills.
  - ○ **Blogs and Articles:** Read blogs and articles to stay up-to-date on the latest trends.
  - ○ **Video Tutorials:** Watch video tutorials to learn visual programming and design techniques.
  - ○ **Example:** Pygame documentation, Panda3D documentation, YouTube

tutorials, online courses on Udemy or Coursera.[29]

- **Open-Source Projects:**
  - ○ **Contribute to Open-Source:** Contribute to open-source game development projects to gain experience and learn from others.
  - ○ **Learn from Code:** Study the source code of open-source projects to learn new techniques.
  - ○ **Example:** Contribute to Pygame, Arcade, or Panda3D projects.
- **Game Jams and Hackathons:**
  - ○ **Participate in Game Jams:** Participate in game jams to build your portfolio and network with other developers.[30]
  - ○ **Learn New Skills:** Game jams provide opportunities to learn new skills and experiment with different game genres.[31]

- o **Example:** Ludum Dare, Global Game Jam, PyWeek.
- **Local Meetups and Events:**
  - o **Attend Meetups:** Attend local meetups and events to network with other developers.
  - o **Share Your Work:** Share your work and get feedback from other developers.
  - o **Example:** Local game development meetups, conferences, and workshops.
- **Educational Institutions:**
  - o **University Courses:** Take university courses in game development or computer science.
  - o **Online Degrees:** Pursue online degrees in game development or related fields.
  - o **Example:** Online degrees from universities or specialized game development schools.
- **Mentorship and Collaboration:**

- **Find a Mentor:** Find a mentor to guide your learning and provide feedback.
- **Collaborate with Others:** Collaborate with other developers on projects to learn from each other.
- **Example:** Join a game development team or find a mentor through online communities.
- **Continuous Learning:**
  - **Stay Updated:** Stay up-to-date on the latest trends and technologies.
  - **Experiment and Explore:** Experiment with different game engines, libraries, and techniques.
  - **Build a Portfolio:** Build a portfolio of your work to showcase your skills.

By actively engaging with the game development community and utilizing available resources, you can accelerate your learning, expand your skillset, and contribute to the future of Python game development.

Conclusion

As we reach the culmination of this exploration into Python game development, it's essential to reflect on the journey we've undertaken and the skills we've acquired. We've traversed the landscape from foundational concepts to advanced techniques, empowering ourselves to create interactive and immersive experiences.

Recap of Key Concepts and Skills Learned: A Foundation for Future Innovation

Throughout this journey, we've covered a diverse range of topics, building a solid foundation for your game development endeavors. Let's recap some of the key concepts and skills we've explored:

- **Python Fundamentals:** We established a strong understanding of Python's syntax, data structures, and control flow, which are essential for any Python-based project.

- **Game Development Libraries:** We delved into popular Python game development libraries like Pygame, Arcade, and Panda3D, each offering unique capabilities for 2D and 3D game creation.

- **2D Game Development:** We explored the creation of 2D games, covering topics such as sprite management, collision detection, and animation.

- **3D Game Development:** We ventured into the realm of 3D game development with Panda3D, learning about 3D modeling, rendering, and physics.[1]

- **User Interface (UI) Design:** We learned how to create intuitive and engaging user interfaces for both 2D and 3D games.

- **Game Logic and State Management:** We mastered the

implementation of game logic and state management, essential for creating complex and dynamic games.

- **Collision Detection and Physics:** We explored techniques for detecting collisions and implementing realistic physics simulations.[2]

- **Animation and Sound:** We learned how to bring games to life with animations and sound effects.

- **Cross-Platform Deployment:** We discovered how to package and distribute games for different operating systems.

- **Game Design Principles:** We explored core game design principles, including level design, storytelling, and monetization strategies.

- **Optimization Techniques:** We learned how to optimize game performance for smooth and responsive gameplay.

- **Emerging Technologies:** We explored the potential of Python in

emerging technologies like VR/AR and cloud gaming.
- **Community and Resources:** We emphasized the importance of community and continuous learning for staying current in the field.

These skills and concepts are not merely theoretical; they are practical tools that you can apply to create your own unique and engaging games.

Encouragement for Continued Exploration and Creation: Igniting Your Passion

The world of game development is vast and ever-evolving. The knowledge and skills you've gained are just the beginning of your journey. I encourage you to continue exploring, experimenting, and creating.
- **Embrace Experimentation:** Don't be afraid to try new techniques, experiment with different game

genres, and push the boundaries of your creativity.

- **Build Your Portfolio:** Create a portfolio of your game projects to showcase your skills to potential employers or collaborators.
- **Participate in Game Jams:** Game jams are a great way to challenge yourself, learn new skills, and network with other developers.[3]
- **Contribute to Open-Source:** Contribute to open-source game development projects to gain experience and give back to the community.
- **Join Online Communities:** Engage with online communities to learn from other developers and share your knowledge.
- **Never Stop Learning:** Stay up-to-date on the latest trends and technologies in game development.

Your passion and dedication are the driving forces behind your success. Embrace the challenges, celebrate the victories, and never stop creating.

The Future of Python Game Development: A Promising Horizon

Python's role in game development is poised to expand significantly in the coming years. Its versatility, ease of use, and growing ecosystem make it well-suited for a variety of applications.

- **AI and Machine Learning:** Python's strong AI and machine learning libraries will play a crucial role in developing intelligent game agents, procedural content generation, and player behavior analysis.[4]
- **Cloud Gaming:** Python's server-side capabilities will be essential for developing cloud gaming services and tools.

- **VR/AR Development:** Python's rapid prototyping and data processing capabilities will make it a valuable tool for VR/AR development.
- **Educational and Indie Games:** Python's accessibility and ease of use will continue to make it a popular choice for educational and indie game development.
- **Tool Development:** Python will remain a go-to language for developing custom tools and automating game development workflows.
- **Metaverse and Emerging Technologies:** Python's adaptability positions it well to contribute to the development of metaverse experiences and other emerging technologies.

The future of Python game development is bright, filled with opportunities for innovation and creativity. By embracing continuous learning and staying connected with the community, you can play a vital role in shaping the future of interactive entertainment.

As you embark on your game development journey, remember that the most important ingredient is your passion. Let your creativity soar, your imagination run wild, and your games inspire and entertain players around the world. The possibilities are endless.

Appendix

This appendix serves as a comprehensive reference guide, providing quick access to essential information and resources for Python game development.

A.1: Python Quick Reference: A Concise Guide to Core Concepts

This section offers a quick reference guide to essential Python concepts, serving as a handy reminder for developers.

- **Data Types:**
    - int: Integers (e.g., 10, -5).
    - float: Floating-point numbers (e.g., 3.14, -0.5).
    - str: Strings (e.g., "Hello", 'World').
    - list: Ordered, mutable sequences (e.g., [1, 2, 3], ['a', 'b', 'c']).
    - tuple: Ordered, immutable sequences (e.g., (1, 2, 3), ('x', 'y', 'z')).

- o dict: Key-value pairs (e.g., {'name': 'John', 'age': 30}).
- o bool: Boolean values (True, False).
- **Control Flow:**
  - o if, elif, else: Conditional statements.
  - o for: Loops for iterating over sequences.
  - o while: Loops that continue as long as a condition is true.
  - o break: Exits a loop.
  - o continue: Skips the current iteration of a loop.
- **Functions:**
  - o def: Defines a function.
  - o return: Returns a value from a function.
  - o lambda: Creates anonymous functions.
- **Modules and Packages:**
  - o import: Imports modules or packages.

- from ... import ...: Imports specific items from a module.
- as: Renames imported items.
- **Exception Handling:**
  - try, except, finally: Handles exceptions.
  - raise: Raises an exception.
- **List Comprehensions:**
  - [expression for item in iterable if condition]: Creates lists concisely.
- **String Formatting:**
  - f-strings: f"Hello, {name}!"
  - .format(): "Hello, {}".format(name)
- **File I/O:**
  - open(): Opens files for reading or writing.
  - read(), write(): Reads and writes data.
- **Object-Oriented Programming (OOP):**
  - class: Defines a class.

- o __init__():   Constructor method.
- o self: Refers to the current object.
- o Inheritance: Creating subclasses.[1]

A.2: Pygame, Arcade, and Panda3D API Summaries: Essential Functionality

This section provides concise summaries of essential API functions for Pygame, Arcade, and Panda3D.

- **Pygame API Summary:**
  - o pygame.init():   Initializes Pygame.
  - o pygame.display.set_mode(): Creates a display surface.
  - o pygame.event.get(): Gets events from the event queue.

- pygame.draw: Functions for drawing shapes.
- pygame.image.load(): Loads images.
- pygame.sprite: Sprite management.
- pygame.mixer: Sound and music.
- pygame.time.Clock: Controls frame rate.

- **Arcade API Summary:**
  - arcade.Window: Creates a window.
  - arcade.Sprite: Manages sprites.
  - arcade.SpriteList: Manages lists of sprites.
  - arcade.draw_*: Functions for drawing shapes.
  - arcade.load_texture(): Loads textures.
  - arcade.play_sound(): Plays sounds.
  - arcade.PhysicsEngineSimple: Simple physics engine.

- o arcade.key: Key constants.
- **Panda3D API Summary:**
  - o ShowBase: Initializes Panda3D.
  - o loader.loadModel(): Loads 3D models.
  - o NodePath: Manages nodes in the scene graph.
  - o render: Root node of the scene graph.
  - o camera: Accesses the camera.
  - o taskMgr: Manages tasks.
  - o CollisionTraverser, CollisionHandlerQueue: Collision detection.
  - o BulletWorld: Physics engine (Bullet).
  - o Shader: Manages shaders.
  - o ParticleSystem: Manages particle systems.
  - o AudioSound: Manages sound.

A.3: Game Asset Resources and Tools: Enhancing Your Creations

This section provides a curated list of resources and tools for creating and acquiring game assets.

- **3D Modeling Tools:**
  - Blender: Free and open-source 3D creation suite.[2]
  - Maya: Industry-standard 3D animation and modeling software.[3]
  - 3ds Max: Professional 3D modeling and animation software.[4]
  - ZBrush: Digital sculpting tool.
- **2D Art and Texture Creation Tools:**
  - GIMP: Free and open-source image editor.[5]
  - Krita: Free and open-source digital painting application.[6]

- o Photoshop: Industry-standard image editing software.[7]
- o Aseprite: Pixel art editor.[8]
- o Substance Painter: 3D texture painting tool.
- **Sound and Music Creation Tools:**
  - o Audacity: Free and open-source audio editor.[9]
  - o LMMS: Free and open-source digital audio workstation.[10]
  - o FL Studio: Professional digital audio workstation.[11]
  - o Bfxr: Sound effect generator.
- **Game Asset Websites:**
  - o Kenney.nl: Free game assets (2D and 3D).[12]
  - o OpenGameArt.org: Free and open-source game assets.
  - o itch.io: Indie game assets and tools.
  - o Unity Asset Store: Paid and free assets for Unity.

- Unreal Engine Marketplace: Paid and free assets for Unreal Engine.
- Sketchfab: 3D models.
- FreeSound.org: Sound effects.
- **Version Control:**
  - Git: Distributed version control system.[13]
  - GitHub: Online platform for Git repositories.
  - GitLab: Online platform for Git repositories.[14]
- **Game Engines and Frameworks:**
  - Godot: Free and open-source game engine.[15]
  - Unity: Cross-platform game engine.[16]
  - Unreal Engine: Powerful game engine.
  - Kivy: Python framework for cross-platform applications.[17]
  - Beeware: Tools to write native applications in python.
- **Level Design Tools:**

- Tiled: General-purpose tile map editor.[18]
- TrenchBroom: Level editor for Quake-engine games.[19]
- **Game Design Documentation Tools:**
  - Google Docs: Online document collaboration.
  - Notion: All-in-one workspace.
  - HackMD: Collaborative markdown editor.[20]
- **AI and Machine Learning Libraries:**
  - TensorFlow: Machine learning library.[21]
  - PyTorch: Machine learning library.[22]
  - Scikit-learn: Machine learning library.[23]
- **Debugging and Profiling Tools:**
  - PDB: Python debugger.[24]
  - RenderDoc: Graphics debugger.
  - Intel VTune Profiler: Performance analysis tool.[25]

This appendix is designed to be a living document, evolving with the Python game development landscape. Remember to explore, experiment, and contribute to the vibrant community that makes Python game development so rewarding.

A.4: Troubleshooting Common Issues

Game development, while a creative and rewarding pursuit, is often a journey through a labyrinth of bugs and errors. This section aims to equip you with the tools and strategies to navigate these challenges effectively.

- **Pygame Troubleshooting: Decoding the Pixelated Puzzles**
  - **"pygame.error: video system not initialized":**
    - This classic error often arises from neglecting the

crucial pygame.init() call. Ensure this function is the very first Pygame command executed in your script.

- Outdated or corrupted display drivers can also trigger this error. Verify your drivers are current and compatible with your operating system.
- If running in a virtual environment, ensure it is activated.

o **"pygame.error: Couldn't open [image/sound]":**

- Double-check file paths for typos and case sensitivity (especially on Linux). Use absolute paths for initial testing.
- Confirm that the file exists in the specified location.

Use relative paths after testing is successful.

- Verify the file format is supported by Pygame (e.g., .png, .jpg, .wav, .ogg).

- If your executable is packaged, ensure that your assets are packaged correctly with it.

○ **Slow Performance: Optimizing the Frame Rate**

- Image optimization is paramount. Resize large images to appropriate dimensions and use compressed formats.

- The pygame.time.Clock object is your ally. Use it to regulate the frame rate and prevent excessive CPU usage.

- Optimize collision detection by using efficient

algorithms and data structures.

- Minimize drawing operations by batching similar elements or using sprite groups.

○ **Sprite Collisions Not Working: Unraveling the Collision Mystery**

- The rect attribute of your sprites is critical for collision detection. Ensure it accurately represents the sprite's dimensions.

- Overlapping sprites can sometimes cause unexpected collision behavior. Use debug visualization to check sprite positions.

- Thoroughly review your collision detection logic. Use print statements or a debugger to trace the flow of execution.

- **Arcade Troubleshooting: Streamlining the Development Process**
  - **"ModuleNotFoundError: No module named 'arcade'":**
    - This error signifies that Arcade is not installed. Use pip install arcade to install it.
    - If using a virtual environment, ensure it is activated.
  - **Blank Screen: Diagnosing the Empty Canvas**
    - Verify that arcade.open_window() and arcade.run() are correctly called. These are essential for displaying the game window.

- Inspect your on_draw() function for errors. Use print statements or a debugger to check for exceptions.
- Make sure that you are calling arcade.start_render() at the begining of your on_draw() function, and arcade.finish_render() at the end of the on_draw() function.

○ **Textures Not Loading: Resolving the Texture Puzzle**
- Double-check file paths and formats. Ensure the texture file is in the correct directory.
- Use arcade.load_texture() to load textures.

○ **Physics Issues: Fine-Tuning the Physical World**

- Verify that the physics engine is correctly initialized using arcade.PhysicsEngineSimple or a more advanced physics engine.
- Check the collision shapes and positions of your sprites.
- Adjust physics parameters such as gravity, friction, and elasticity to achieve desired effects.

- **Panda3D Troubleshooting: Taming the 3D Beast**
  - **"ImportError: No module named panda3d.core":**
    - This error indicates that Panda3D is not properly installed. Reinstall Panda3D and ensure the environment variables are correctly set.

- Verify that the python interpreter that you are using, is the one that panda3d is installed into.
- **Black Screen or No Model Displayed: Illuminating the 3D Void**
  - Verify that the model is loaded using loader.loadModel() and reparented to render.
  - Check for errors in the model file using a 3D modeling tool.
  - Ensure the camera is correctly positioned and that lighting is properly set up.
- **Shader Errors: Deciphering the Shader Code**
  - Check the shader code for syntax errors using a GLSL validator.

- Verify that the shader is loaded using Shader.load() and applied using node.setShader().
- Use Panda3D's shader debugging tools, such as setShaderInput() to pass data to the shader and getShaderInput() to retrieve it.
  - **Physics Issues: Mastering the Physics Simulation**
    - Verify that the physics world is created using BulletWorld or PhysXWorld and that objects are added using attachRigidBody().
    - Check the collision shapes and positions of your rigid bodies.
    - Adjust physics parameters such as gravity, mass, and

friction to achieve desired effects.

- ○ **Performance Issues: Optimizing the 3D World**
  - Use Panda3D's profiling tools, such as the built-in frame rate meter and task timer, to identify bottlenecks.[1]
  - Optimize models by reducing polygon count and using LODs.
  - Optimize textures by using compressed formats and mipmapping.
  - Optimize shaders by reducing complexity and minimizing texture sampling.
  - Adjust render settings, such as anti-aliasing and shadow quality, to balance visual quality and performance.

- **General Troubleshooting Tips: The Developer's Arsenal**
  - **Read Error Messages Carefully:** Error messages are your first line of defense. Decipher their meaning and use them as clues.
  - **Use Print Statements:** Strategically placed print() statements can help you track variable values and debug code flow.
  - **Use a Debugger:** A debugger (e.g., PDB) allows you to step through code, inspect variables, and set breakpoints.[2]
  - **Simplify the Problem:** Break down complex problems into smaller, manageable parts.
  - **Search Online:** Leverage the vast resources of online forums, documentation, and Stack Overflow.

- ○ **Ask for Help:** Don't hesitate to seek assistance from online communities or experienced developers.

A.5: Glossary of Game Development Terms: Deciphering the Developer's Lexicon

This glossary provides definitions of common game development terms, helping you navigate the technical jargon.

- **Alpha Blending:** A technique for combining images with transparency.
- **Animation Blending:** Smoothly transitioning between animations.
- **Aspect Ratio:** The ratio of the width to the height of an image or screen.
- **Billboard:** A 2D image or sprite that always faces the camera.

- **Bump Mapping:** A technique for simulating surface details using a heightmap.
- **Collision Mask:** A bitmask used to define which objects collide with each other.
- **Deferred Shading:** A rendering technique that separates lighting and shading calculations.
- **Delta Time:** The time elapsed between frames, used to ensure consistent game speed.
- **Gimbal Lock:** A problem that occurs when using Euler angles to represent rotations.[3]
- **Interpolation:** A technique for estimating values between known data points.[4]
- **Kinematic Body:** A physics body that is moved directly by code, not by forces.
- **Normal Map:** A texture that stores surface normals, used for bump mapping.[5]

- **Occlusion Culling:** A technique for preventing rendering of hidden objects.
- **Particle System:** A technique for creating visual effects using a large number of small particles.[6]
- **Quaternion:** A mathematical representation of rotations, used to avoid gimbal lock.[7]
- **Ray Tracing:** A rendering technique that simulates the path of light rays.
- **Rigid Body:** A physics body that is affected by forces and collisions.
- **Scripting Language:** A programming language used to control game logic.[8]
- **Texture Atlas:** A single texture that contains multiple smaller textures.[9]
- **Vertex Shader:** A shader that processes vertex data.[10]
- **Fragment Shader:** A shader that processes pixel data.

- **WASM (WebAssembly):** A binary instruction format for stack-based virtual machines.

www.ingramcontent.com/pod-product-compliance
Lightning Source LLC
La Vergne TN
LVHW051420050326
832903LV00030BC/2919